Gerard P. Weber and Robert Miller

Breaking Open the Gospel of John

St. Anthony Messenger Press
Cincinnati, Ohio

Nihil Obstat: Rev. Hilarion Kistner, O.F.M.
Rev. Edward L. Gratsch

Imprimi Potest: Rev. John Bok, O.F.M.
Provincial

Imprimatur: +Most Reverend Carl K. Moeddel, V.G.
Archdiocese of Cincinnati
May 12, 1995

The *nihil obstat* and *imprimatur* are a declaration that a book
is considered to be free from doctrinal or moral error. It is
not implied that those who have granted the *nihil obstat*
and *imprimatur* agree with the contents, opinions or
statements expressed.

Scripture citations are taken from the *New Revised Standard
Version Bible,* copyright ©1989 by the Division of Christian
Education of the National Council of the Churches of
Christ in the U.S.A., and used by permission.

The excerpt from *John,* by Gerard Sloyan, copyright ©1988
by John Knox Press, is reprinted by permission of
Westminster Press.

The excerpt from *Sheppy,* by Somerset Maugham,
copyright ©1933 by William Heinemann Ltd., is reprinted
in the United Kingdom and Canada by permission of Reed
Consumer Books.

Cover and book design by Julie Lonneman

Illustration by Stephen D. Kroeger and Julie Lonneman

ISBN 0-86716-219-8

Copyright ©1995, Gerard P. Weber and Robert Miller

All rights reserved.

Published by St. Anthony Messenger Press
Printed in the U.S.A.

Contents

Introduction

T HE SUN WAS SINKING SLOWLY into the ocean, the tide imperceptibly receding. The roses, daisies and bougainvillea were drowsily swaying in the gentle breeze. A poet with a touch of the mystic in him and a friend with a scientific, pragmatic, nuts-and-bolts type of mind sat in the garden nestled next to a seawall, silently watching the scene. Each saw the same sights. Yet each was touched in a different way. The poet instinctively felt the breeze as the hand of God stroking his cheek and saw in the beauty of the flowers and in the expanse of the ocean the grandeur of God. The scientist reflected on the power of the sun and on the fact that, big and brilliant as it was, it was still only a minor star in the universe. She attributed the breeze to the nightly change of temperature and reflected on the long evolutionary process that resulted in such different types of flowers. In time she, too, worked her way through to the grandeur of God because she recognized order and power in nature.

The mix of poet and scientist in each of us is varied. In no two people is it exactly alike. Each will bring his or her mixture to the Gospel of John. The person with a strong poetic bent will read the Prologue and the sermons of Jesus and be drawn into soaring, whirling, twisting images of God.

John speaks of a Word of power flowing from the mouth of God to tame the chaos of the waters that covered the world, a Word that brought forth the sun and the flowers as well as each human being. He sings of a Word of love who leaps from the sky and settles down among weak, fallen, frightened, bewildered human beings—a Word who, when absorbed into believing hearts, sweeps people up into a higher level of life and reality. Poets will feel the impact of darkness upon people who refuse to accept the light; they will feel the warmth that comes when the dawn breaks. They will see dark and cold creeping in as the sun slowly recedes and slinking away when a fire is kindled. When poets read John's words aloud warmth, feeling, excitement will ring in their voice.

People with a more scientific and empirical bent of mind will be drawn to the words on the page and will try to analyze and organize the meaning of these so that they become clear and definite in their minds. They will want to go back to the original Greek to find why John calls Jesus the Word. They will want to know what the Greek philosophers meant by *Logos* (word) and why John chose that particular word to sum up the divine nature of Christ. People who are very logical or literal in their thinking will trace the many other words, phrases and events John uses to demonstrate that Jesus, the Christ, is the Son of God. These they will lay out in an orderly pattern so they can move step by step to a declaration of faith.

Sister Rose Therese had a poetic soul that caught the message of John's images and symbolism. Nicknamed "Twinkle Toes" because she had such zest for life and showed so much joy in teaching, she spoke of God in poetic language with vivid images from nature. A religious for only a quarter of a century, she was not yet fifty when she lay dying from cancer.

Her last conscious act was to ask the sisters gathered at her bedside to put down their rosaries and read the Gospel of John to her. She whispered, "I have tried to live my life by that Gospel. I want to die with it." The sister who picked up the Bible had not read many pages before Rose met the Jesus whom John proclaimed.

People who, like Sister Rose Therese, have a more

poetical and mystical bent, will read the Gospel of John and soar on the wings of signs, symbols and poetic allusions to the very throne of the One whose appearance gleams like jasper and carnelian.

Others who pick up this Gospel may not be able to soar. More accustomed to taking words and events at face value, they are like the carpenter who did finishing work on the Marin County Civic Center north of San Francisco. The last building designed by Frank Lloyd Wright, it straddles two small hillocks. The color of the brick and stone, the bright roof, the curves of the many arches and the sweep of the balconies blend the building into the landscape. Architects and artists admire the breadth of Wright's vision and the beauty of the building. The carpenter hardly noticed its lines. For him it was just another job. Yet as he laid floors and hung doors he began to feel the harmony and beauty of that building. His attitude slowly changed. One Sunday he proudly brought his children out to show them the floor that Daddy had laid and the doors he had hung. He saw the beauty of that building from his own individual perspective.

People with this more pragmatic, empirical bent of mind will prefer to look at the historical background of the events, the history of the text, the original meaning of the words, the differences in texts and translations as well as the meaning behind the text. They will look at the pages through eyes accustomed to the literal meaning of words and to a more orderly and logical presentation of a message. These will find their way to the throne of God by ranging through details and background material. They merely take different paths to faith.

Both of these approaches, poetic/mystical and philosophical/exegetical, help us reach out to the God whom Jesus came to reveal. They help us break open the Gospel of John. Some people will favor one. Some will favor the other. Most will use a bit of both at different times. The poetic/mystical approach will most often be found in the works of the great mystics. The theological/exegetical approach can be found in more scholarly commentaries such as the Anchor Bible. These take time and effort to read and are not very inspiring. Many popular and less detailed commentaries blend the two approaches, symbolism and poetry, with scholarly explanations of the text.

Perspectives on the Gospel

Before we climb aboard the wings of the eagle that is the traditional symbol for John, it would be good to set this Gospel in perspective with a few questions. First, who was this man John? There is no doubt that he was a mystic and a contemplative, but scholars do not agree on who he was. Some identify him as an eyewitness of the events. Others follow an early tradition that he was John, son of Zebedee, the beloved disciple. Still others say he was simply an author who followed the acceptable practice of the time and attributed his work to John the apostle. In the long run it makes little difference who actually put words on parchment. The Church, by accepting the Gospel of John as divinely inspired, has declared the book to be an authentic and reliable guide to the meaning of Jesus' life, death and resurrection.

Second, for whom was this Gospel written? Again scholars cannot with certainty identify the Christian community that gave birth to this Gospel or the exact time it took its final form. The introduction to this Gospel in the *New American Bible* says: "The final editing of the gospel and arrangement in its present form probably dates from between A.D. 90 and 100. Traditionally, Ephesus has been favored as the place of composition, though many support a location in Syria, perhaps the city of Antioch, while others have suggested other places, including Alexandria."

Again, it really matters little for whom and when the book was written. Its message is timeless, one that speaks to us today. Its importance lies in our response in faith when we

4

read it and in the effect it has on the way we see God, Jesus and life.

Third, what is the structure of this Gospel? Many commentators divide the Gospel into two parts. They call the first part after the Prologue (John 1:19—12:50) the Book of Signs because these chapters contain the miracles or signs Jesus worked so that those who followed him might believe in him. They call the second part (John 13—20) the Book of Glory because it comes to a climax in Jesus' glorification in the last week of his life. They see John 21 as a later addition. Other commentators disagree with this division because Jesus' greatest sign is his death and resurrection, which is not in the Book of Signs.

Whether John had a definite, logical plan in writing the Gospel cannot be easily discerned from the text. We have to remember that he wrote a text from beginning to end and did not put in titles and subheads as we do. Neither did he put in chapter and verse numbers. (These were added in the thirteenth century but not printed in the text until the sixteenth century.) Another reason why it is not easy to identify a clear structure is that John uses symbols to hint at a deeper reality and repeats them in various ways in various parts of the book. His book may be seen as a swirling whirlwind that begins spread out over a wide area and gradually funnels down to one point when it touches the ground. In John that point is Jesus, the Son of God who reveals to us what God is like. Thus the book has to be read time and time again, reflected on frequently and appreciated only when it all comes together in a grand "Aha! That's who Jesus is! That's what God is like!"

Fourth, how is this Gospel similar to or different from the other three Gospels? A cursory perusal of it will show that it is much different from the Synoptic Gospels (Matthew, Mark and Luke). In fact, some scholars wonder whether John even had a copy of the Synoptics at hand. John's view of Jesus is much different from theirs: He stresses Jesus' divinity, power and authority in a way the other

5

Gospel writers do not.

John's order of events is different from that found in Matthew, Mark or Luke. He tells few of the miracles and sayings the others have in common. Scholars usually list only seven signs in John—transforming water into wine at Cana, curing the royal official's son, healing the sick man at the pool of Bethesda, multiplying the loaves and fishes, walking on the water, healing the man born blind and raising Lazarus from the dead. (The ancients viewed seven as a number symbolic of perfection. Perhaps John means to indicate that these seven signs are sufficient for coming to believe that Jesus is the Messiah, the Son of God.) Of these miracles four (Cana, Bethesda, the man born blind and Lazarus) are unique to John.

These differences should not surprise us too much. Because the Gospels are works of theology, not history or biography, we should expect that the understanding of Jesus would develop and deepen with time. John's Gospel has the most advanced theology of them all. He wrote sometime around the end of the first century, as much as thirty or forty years after the other three had completed their stories of Jesus. He recorded in narrative and incident the insights of his community into the divine nature of Christ, which was not as clearly defined when the earlier Synoptics wrote.

Finally, we may ask, "Why did John write his Gospel?" He himself answers this question in his poetic Prologue:

> In the beginning was the Word, and the Word was with God and the Word was God.... And the Word became flesh and lived among us, and we have seen his glory, the glory as of a father's only son, full of grace and truth.... [T]o all who received, who believed in his name, him he gave power to become children of God (1:1, 14, 12).

To make sure that his readers do not miss the point of his narrative, John repeats his purpose at the end of his Gospel:

Now Jesus did many other signs in the presence of his disciples, which are not written in this book. But these are written that you may come to believe that Jesus is the Messiah, the Son of God, and that through believing you may have life in his name (20:30-31).

With this ending John seems to be calling for an "Aha!" from the reader. Something like: "So that's what it's all about; that's what is important for me to hear in this story; that's what I am to get from reading this Gospel. Like Thomas I will not persist in my unbelief but will be able to cry out 'My Lord and my God!' and embrace a new kind of life."

How to Use This Book

This book is meant to be read slowly, a bit at a time, along with reflection on pages from John's Gospel. At the beginning of each section in this book the pertinent chapter and verses of John's Gospel are indicated. If you are not familiar with the passage, read the selection before reading the text. If you are familiar with it, it may be more helpful to read the Scripture selection after reading the text but before beginning the Reflection.

At the end of each section are questions for reflection to help you see your experiences and thoughts in the light of the God whom Jesus reveals. Frequently they will ask in some way: "What does this passage reveal about the God who became flesh?" At other times they will probe "What does this selection suggest about my life experiences?" You may not always be able to give a clear and easy answer to these questions, but raising and considering them is crucial to breaking open the Gospel of John.

Although the book can be helpful for individual reading and reflection, it is better to read and reflect on it in a small group. The members of the group can then share their ideas and have the support of the group in finding the meaning of the Gospel story for their lives. It is important in small group discussions that the members do not argue about the meaning of a passage, try to correct another's ideas or lecture about the background of the passage. By questions and suggestions, however, the members may help one other clarify their thoughts and see more clearly the connection between their lives and the Gospel. It is also helpful if the group members read the material ahead of time and think about their answers to the questions.

PRAYER

A short prayer for guidance and understanding,
something like this, is a good beginning for each session:

Lord, open my mind to the words and deeds of Jesus.
Inflame my heart with love for him.
Guide me to faith in him
    and help me to live the new life he offers.
This we ask in Jesus' name. Amen.

FOR REFLECTION

1) *When you read or listen to the Gospel of John, do you*
    tend to be more like the poet or the scientist?

2) *What do you hope to get from reading about and*
    discussing this Gospel?

Chapter One

The Prologue

THE IMPACT OF THE POETIC APPROACH is illustrated by the story of how the faith of a woman we will call Jane was ignited by this Gospel. She has a strong poetic soul. For her the Gospel of John is the window through which she sees God. But it was not always so. In her twenties she stepped out of the Church and cast aside the image of God garnered from her childhood: a Father who was a stern judge, a Son who was a spoilsport handing out too many prohibitions and a Spirit who floated around disguised as a dove.

During the tumultuous years of the sixties she was involved in an interracial dialogue. Hearing one day of a weekend ecumenical workshop on human rights, she talked a neighbor into caring for her children and went to the workshop. At the end of one session a Methodist minister read a passage from Scripture. "God is love," she heard, "and those who abide in love abide in God, and God abides in them" (1 John 4:16b). The passage struck her so forcefully that she later said that it was the first credible thing she had heard anyone say about God.

She went home and read the Gospel of John backward and forward looking for the quote but could not find it. (At the time she did not know that three letters attributed to John are also part of the Bible.) From her repeated reading of this Gospel an image of a good and loving God emerged so strongly that she said, "That is the kind of God I can believe in!"

Today she glows with excitement when she quotes the Prologue of John's Gospel. She insists that it says more to her about the love and grandeur of God than any book of theology or spirituality. For her John's metaphors of light and darkness, of a living Word, of the bread of life, are the mirrors in which she sees God indistinctly while waiting to see God face-to-face.

To have the Prologue of this Gospel touch our lives we have to do what the old-time preacher said he was going to do as he climbed into the pulpit: "I'm going to ponder the imponderable, explain the unexplainable, define the indefinable and scrutinize the inscrutable." This daunting task is accomplished not merely by analyzing text and words but also by letting our imagination open our minds and hearts to John's poetry so that we can know the God who is indefinable, ponder the mystery of a Word made flesh and scrutinize the inexplicable gift of divine life Jesus offers us.

The Word Made Flesh (John 1:14)

John takes our imaginations on a dizzy ride in the first nineteen verses of his Gospel. We mount a flaming chariot harnessed to flaming horses similar to the one that took Elijah to heaven (see 2 Kings 2:11) and hurtle between heaven and earth, between eternity and the present with the speed of light.

John begins by plunging back eons before time began to find the Word of God already there. "In the beginning was the Word, and the Word was with God and the Word was God" (1:1). Then he hurtles into a time warp, and has the Word creating not only the forms of life we know, not only the world we know, but everything that exists in those galaxies billions of light years away on the edge of nothingness. "All things came into being through him, and without him not one thing came into being" (1:3a).

We pause and catch our breath, recalling the opening

story in the Bible: "In the beginning...God created the heavens and the earth.... Then God said, 'Let there be light.... Let the earth bring forth living creatures of every kind.... Let us make humankind in our image, according to our likeness....' " (Genesis 1:1a, 3a, 24b, 26b).

The chariot races on, but John slows it to pause at one particular point in history, around 3 or 4 B.C., when the Word pitched his tent on earth, when the eternal became present in a unique way at a particular time and place. John wants to make it clear that the Word of God became truly human; Jesus was not just a divine being pretending to act and talk like a man. "And the Word became flesh and lived among us, and we have seen his glory, the glory as of a father's only son, full of grace and truth" (1:14).

After the Prologue, John's chariot picks up speed and races through a number of years, perhaps thirty. It pulls up at the time when John the Baptizer points out Jesus as the Son of God. Slowly the chariot moves ahead through the next three years, until finally John says that he cannot put down all the signs that Jesus did, but that "these are written so that you may come to believe that Jesus is the Messiah, the Son of God, and that through believing you may have life in his name" (20:31).

But this is not the end of the ride. The chariot races across two thousand years and John pulls up his powerful steeds to ask each one who picks up his book, "Would you like to continue on this ride with me to find what it means to be fully human, what your life can be, what the life being offered to those who believe in Jesus is like?"

If we wish to ride with John through the pages of his Gospel we need to stop along the way and reflect on the events, the metaphors, the symbols he uses. For example, John calls Jesus the Word of God. We need to mull over the way Jesus is like a word. He is called that only three times in Scripture—and all three are in this Prologue. Yet it is a most appropriate description of him. A word is a means of communication, and Jesus certainly is God's greatest

11

communication to human beings, because Jesus is more than a message from God. He *is* God.

Words reveal something about the speaker. The Word of God does more than that. He reveals the very nature of God because he is God. He himself says, "Whoever has seen me has seen the Father" (John 14:9c). Thus, in a very real way, when we see and hear Jesus, we are actually seeing and hearing God.

John uses the Greek word *Logos*, which implies more than communication. *Logos* also contains the idea of order and reason. Jesus certainly came to bring order and reason into an unreasonable world torn by chaos. A word can clarify a situation, help one see life differently, bring understanding where there was none before.

A word has power. It can calm a frightened child or launch a war. It can move one to friendship or enmity. A word can give life when hope has died and a heart is cold. Originally the Word of God gave physical life to human beings, but now he renews that life, and freely bestows a new life, a better life, on those who hear and accept him.

John uses another metaphor to convey the same truth: He writes that Jesus is the *light* that shines in the darkness. He is like a lighthouse at the entrance of a harbor, indicating where safety and security from the storms of life can be found. Those who hear the Word and accept the light are given the power to become children of God.

When we read the portrait of Jesus painted by John we need to be conscious that on a deeper level we are seeing a portrait of God. Our interpretation and understanding of this Gospel should go something like this: "Jesus is God, and Jesus is kind and merciful, loving and forgiving, just and understanding. Therefore, God is kind and merciful, loving and forgiving, just and understanding."

To this we have to add, "But Jesus is also human. Therefore, he had the very human limitations of time and place. He could not preach to everyone in the world. He could not cure all the sick. He faced rejection by many of those for whom he cared, even betrayal by a close friend. He died, just as we will. In Jesus we see what God is like and we see what it means to be fully human, to be a child of a heavenly Father."

This Prologue, like the rest of the Gospel, has to be read time and time again to ponder the imponderable. It cannot be grasped in one reading, by studying one book, by attending one class. Each time you approach it something new waits in the metaphors and symbols, something deeper and richer in the words. The person with a poetic bent of mind will do well to savor the images and allow them to speak. The person with the more logical, orderly, empirical bent of mind will do well to read the footnotes, look up the references and consult a good commentary.

FOR REFLECTION

1) *What does John's Prologue suggest to you about God and about God's relationship with human beings?*

2) *What do the words* word *and* light *suggest to you about the kind of person Jesus is and the kind of God our God is?*

Light and Life

John Donne, a seventeenth-century English clergyman and poet, told a story about a man who was searching for God. One day, the story goes, this man got the idea that God lived on top of a high mountain at the far end of the world. So he set out to find the mountain and climb it. After a long, difficult, dangerous journey through dense jungles and dismal swamps, the man arrived at the mountain. As the man looked up—and up and up—he realized that the mountain was higher and steeper than he had imagined. But because he wanted to find God more than anything else, he carefully studied the four sides of the mountain for the best possible route to the top. He decided to climb the east wall. At the crack of dawn the next morning he set out.

It so happened that God did indeed live on the top of that mountain. On the very day when the man started up the rocky slope God thought, "I love my people so much. What can I do to show them my great love?" Then God got an idea: "I will leave this mountaintop and go down and live among my people as one of them." God looked down the four sides of the mountain and decided that the quickest descent would be by the west wall. Next morning at the crack of dawn God started down the west wall.

And so, as luck would have it, the two passed on opposite sides of the mountain. After a long and perilous climb the man reached the summit and found it empty. Weary and discouraged, he thought, "God does not live here after all. Maybe God does not exist at all. If he does exist, and he does not live on the top of this mountain, where does he live?" The man fell on his face and began to weep. After a good cry he sat up and said to himself, "Why should I go back down the dangerous trail to my village? There is nothing there but poor ignorant people. It would be far better to stay on top of this mountain alone then to go back there."

At this point John Donne ended his story, but John the Evangelist suggests an ending for us. God traveled faster down the mountain than the man who was climbing up it. He was already settled in among the poor and ignorant people when he heard the man's agonized question. God looked up to the top of the mountain and called, "My son. I do exist. Here I am down in the village among those poor and ignorant people. Come down and share my life with me and with these, my children and friends."

We are the people searching for God. Often we look in faraway places when actually God is a villager living close by, a carpenter, one very much like us who wishes very much to share a life with us. In his writings John is the voice of God calling us to come and share in the divine life.

The call comes through the signs John records. At the end of the Gospel he says that there are not enough books written to contain all the wonderful things Jesus did. The nature of the life we are offered is revealed in the symbolic language John uses. For example, in the Prologue John compares this new life to light: "What has come into being in him was life, and the life was the light of all people" (1:3b-4).

This life is like a treasure. It is something we all desire and want to have to the fullest, but what kind of life is John taking about? We know of all sorts of life—from that of the virus that causes a common cold to that of a genius like Beethoven. But what is this life Jesus speaks of and how is it different from the life our parents gave us? As we read, it becomes clear that this life is sharing in the life of Jesus. Not only does Jesus share our human life with us; we also share his divine life with him.

The treasure is the gift of friendship with God. It is finding God and sharing God's life! This we do when we embrace Jesus:

> If you know me, you will know my Father also. From now on you do know him and have seen him.... Whoever has seen me has seen the Father.... Believe me that I am in the Father and the Father is in me... (14:7, 9c, 11a).

FOR REFLECTION

1) *Where and how have you searched for God in your life?*

2) *What does John Donne's story suggest to you about where to look for God?*

3) *What images, ideas or questions come to your mind when you hear or read the word* life *in the Gospel?*

4) *What does sharing in the life of God mean to you?*

Chapter Two

The Call to Faith and Discipleship

T HE BIBLE DESCRIBES GOD calling people in dramatic ways. Abram had a vision: "Go from your country and your kindred and your father's house to the land that I will show you" (Genesis 12:1b). Moses's encounter with God was even more dramatic: "...[T]he angel of the Lord appeared to him in a flame of fire out of a bush" (Exodus 3:2a). Jeremiah heard the call of God, but resisted it and had to be reassured that God would be with him (see Jeremiah 1:4-19). Isaiah saw "the Lord sitting on a throne, high and lofty; and the hem of his robe filled the temple" (Isaiah 6:1b). After all these dramatic precedents, we would have expected a thunderous call when the Son of God first called two men to follow him. Instead the call came in a simple quiet invitation, "Come and see" (see John 1:35-39).

The God whom Jesus came to reveal is not the God of thunder and lightning before whom one must remove one's shoes, the sight of whose face can kill. This is a gentle God, calling, coaxing, offering life but never coercing. The evangelist pictures how God-made-man used the gentle approach to arouse the curiosity of the first disciples. John the Baptizer, son of Elizabeth and Zechariah, was preaching by the Jordan. He was filled with the zeal of the Lord, but he also had to deny vigorously and vociferously that he was the

Messiah, Elijah returned from heaven or even the prophet foretold by Moses (see Deuteronomy 18:18). He claimed that he was merely a voice crying in the wilderness pointing the way. He stood at the crossroads of time. His outstretched arms pointed in two directions. With one arm he pointed to the past, to Moses and the law, to the life the people had forsaken. With the other arm he pointed to the future, to the Lamb of God who is the promise of new life.

'What Are You Looking For?' (John 1:35-51)

John's words about Jesus aroused the curiosity of Andrew and his companion, whom most commentators think was the apostle John, and they took the road to the future. They wanted to know more about the one upon whom the Baptist had seen a dove descend, the one whom he had recognized as the Lamb of God. Their journey to a new life began when Jesus responded to their curiosity by asking them a question: "What are you looking for?" (1:38b).

The two disciples did not answer directly. They countered his question by asking another: "Rabbi, where are you staying?" Obviously, they wanted to know more than Jesus' home address. Perhaps they did not know what they were really looking for. Were they merely curious to learn more about this new teacher? Did they perhaps hope that he might be the Messiah who would free them from the Romans? Were they seeking enlightenment about Moses and the law? Was there an emptiness in their lives, a longing in their hearts for something more?

We can only surmise that they approached Jesus looking for more than information. Consciously or unconsciously, they were seeking to satisfy a longing in their hearts for something more than they had. As a result they were open to something new.

Jesus responded to their question about where he was staying by inviting them to come and see. This Andrew and

John did. The Gospel story tells us nothing about what was said at that meeting. But in their conversation with Jesus they must have sensed that he liked them—not only from what he said but from the tone of his voice, his gestures, the light in his eyes. They connected. They hit it off. They stayed with him the rest of the day. Trust and faith in Jesus were born.

In fact, Andrew and John were so taken with Jesus that they went off and told others about him. Andrew recruited his brother Simon, whom Jesus renamed Peter. Andrew's companion recruited his brother, James. The next day, when Jesus invited Philip to follow him, he too invited another—his friend Nathanael—to join their little band.

What was it that caught these men's attention and moved them to walk with Jesus? John does not answer that question directly. But he does tell the stories of a few of those who followed Jesus when he walked the hills of Palestine. From their stories we can deduce three stages in discipleship.

The first stage is curiosity: interest in and fascination with the person of Jesus. The second is actual discipleship, that is, joining the band of believers, listening to and learning from Jesus. The third is friendship: intimacy with Jesus and with his Father, the discovery of the true treasure.

John makes it clear that many more people than those first six disciples were curious about Jesus. People came long distances to see and hear Jesus. They were fascinated by him and by his message; they followed him.

From Darkness Into Light

But fascination is only the first step in acquiring the life Jesus offers. Many of the people who were intrigued by Jesus and who listened to him did not become disciples. They found his message too hard to believe. Andrew and John, along with Peter and James, Philip and Nathanael took the second step: They spent time in the company of Jesus, learning from him about the new life he had come to give.

They gradually got to know him. Without realizing it, they were getting to know God as well.

Gradually they became more and more enthralled with Jesus' vision of life. They saw their lives and the future in a different light. They dreamed the kind of dreams the prophet said young men would have (see Joel 2:28). Life could be and would be different. Knowing Jesus, they acquired a new and exciting vision of God.

But the evangelist in short order indicates that not everyone's curiosity led them immediately to go see what Jesus had to offer. Some resisted the attraction of Jesus. Nathanael had a closed mind when Philip approached him (1:45-51). He could not see beyond his prejudice; he could not conceive that anything worthwhile could come out of Nazareth, a small, out-of-the-way village just a few miles from his hometown of Cana. Before Nathanael's mind and heart opened to Jesus, Jesus had to manifest his power by revealing that he knew Nathanael's most secret thoughts.

Throughout the Gospel there are people who hold back from Jesus' invitation—people who have a closed mind, a closed heart or both. Jesus spoke of these people as living in darkness and working at night. He spoke of those who were fascinated by him and who followed him as living in light and working during the day.

The God whom Jesus reveals seems too good to be true. Unlike the distant, all-powerful God whom people revere and stand in awe of, the God Jesus reveals lives and acts with humanity in the most extraordinary ordinary way. This God is gentle, concerned, forgiving and loving. This God often makes an offer of a new kind of life indirectly through a human being—John the Baptizer, for one. This God desires to be with ordinary people in preference to the rich and powerful. The God of whom Jesus is the image has great respect for human freedom. Those called have to accept the call freely. They can, if they wish, walk away; they can even betray God.

Andrew and John, along with the other disciples,

reached a third and final third stage in their relationship with Jesus when, at the Last Supper, he called them friends and washed their feet. Curiosity had led them to follow Jesus; living with him and listening to him had given them a new vision of God and of new life. But at the Last Supper they acquired a new vision of themselves. They were not slaves or servants, but friends of Jesus, friends of God. The third and final stage of their relationship with Jesus was intimate friendship with him. This friendship with Jesus also meant getting to know God as Jesus knew him.

"What are you looking for?" is a question addressed not only to two curious young men. It is a question that Jesus through John asks each person who picks up this Gospel. It is not an easy question to answer. We are prone to confuse our wants with our needs.

The *Reader's Digest* once related a story about a little girl who asked her father for the doll in the store window. He told her that she did not need another doll because she already had three fairly new dolls. Then he explained the difference between wants and needs. When he finished, she said, "Daddy, when I want something I need it."

What we think we want from Jesus may not be what we need and what we need from him may not be what we want from him. Whatever our reason for being curious about Jesus and for being fascinated with him, the important thing is to get to know him by thoughtful, prayerful study of the gospel and to become a disciple. The end result will be friendship with him and a new vision of God and of ourselves.

FOR REFLECTION

1) What "John the Baptizers" in your life have pointed you toward Jesus? What did they say or do?

2) What does the story of the call of the first disciples suggest to you about the way God calls you?

Water Becomes Vintage Wine (John 2:1-12)

Belief did not come any easier to the disciples than it does for us. They needed some sort of sign to help them recognize and accept Jesus for who he was. John writes that the first of the signs Jesus did to reveal his glory and so lead his disciples to believe in him was to transform plain, ordinary water into vintage wine at a wedding feast. By putting this story, so rich in symbolism, at the beginning of his Gospel John is calling upon his readers also to see the glory of Jesus and to believe in him.

But to see beyond the fact that Jesus was compassionate to a host who had run out of drinks for his guests or that he loved and heeded his mother, it is necessary to look beyond the obvious meaning of Jesus' words and actions and find the deeper reality hidden under this sign.

It is easy to recognize the meaning of a sign when we know what it intends to communicate. Thus an outstretched arm with the palm of the hand held up means stop or slow down. A sweep of the arm across the body from one side or the other means go ahead. In John, a sign is a way of saying something about Jesus through a miraculous event. But when a sign's symbolic meaning is not clearly recognized, we need to figure out its deeper meaning.

Our reflection can begin by relating the action or story to our experience. Thus, while reading this story of the wedding at Cana we recall not only the good food and drink we have had at weddings but also the joy, the excitement, the friendship, the pleasure of those weddings.

If we stop there the symbolic meaning is minimal. The richness of a symbolic action in Scripture grows when memories such as these lead people to search for other Scripture passages that speak about wine, such as Isaiah's vision of the coming day of the Lord:

> On this mountain the LORD of hosts will make for all
>   peoples
>   a feast of rich food, a feast of well-aged wines,
>   of rich food filled with marrow,
>   of well-aged wines strained clear (Isaiah 25:6).

Thus this miracle gains depth and meaning that goes beyond the event itself because it shows that a new age was beginning with Jesus.

Another path to follow in looking for the deeper meaning of the wedding feast is to look at individual items in the story to see what they reveal about Jesus and about the nature of God. For example, the amount and the kind of wine is highly symbolic of the prodigality of God's concern for our needs. Jesus did not produce a case or two of ordinary wine, just enough to tide the bridegroom over. He transformed six water jars, each holding *twenty or thirty gallons,* into vintage wine. Seeing what Jesus did, we see that God responds to our needs in a most generous and lavish way.

Still another way to delve into the symbolic meaning of this story is to read it from the viewpoint of other significant but mysterious changes which occur in the lives of those who believe. For example, the transformation of water into wine suggests that Baptism, through the power of Christ, changes ordinary human life into something rich and wonderful even while that life seems to remain basically the same.

At Cana the water in the jars was not done away with. It was not thrown out. It was transformed. The good wine that the headwaiter tasted was still mostly the same water that had been in the jars, but it had been changed. Wine is mostly water, drawn from the earth and from the sky into the vine. There the live vine changes the water into juice that will, through the human effort of crushing, fermenting and aging, become wine.

The new life given by Jesus and symbolized by the wine is not a transformation into an otherworldly kind of life. It is the same life we always have had transformed into the "best" kind of life, one that is lived in and with and through him. The potential for being a better person (a new wine) has always been present in us, but it has to be activated by Jesus. Through faith and Baptism we are drawn into the living vine, Jesus. In this union something is added that, through the crushing and fermentation process of daily living, transforms ordinary human life into something divine.

This reality is beautifully expressed when a few drops of water are added to the wine during the Preparation of the Gifts at the Eucharist: "By the mystery of this water and wine may we come to share in the divinity of Christ, who humbled himself to share in our humanity." The process by which this transformation takes place is expressed in the next prayer:

> Blessed are you, Lord, God of all creation.
> Through your goodness we have this wine to offer,
> fruit of the vine and work of human hands.
> It will become our spiritual drink.

Both the power of God and human activity are needed if the life Jesus offers is to take root, grow and flourish.

The changing of water into wine also brings to mind the Last Supper and our celebration of the Eucharist, in which Jesus takes ordinary bread and wine and changes them into his Body and Blood. Through the centuries many people have questioned whether the bread and the wine actually become the Body and Blood of Christ. They have wondered how this could be. Their senses tell them that the bread still looks like bread and that the wine still tastes like wine. Surveys show that even many Catholics think that the bread and wine are only symbolic representations of Christ. Reflecting on the wedding feast at Cana does not answer the *how* of this transformation, but it certainly bolsters faith in the power of Christ to change one substance into another.

1) How would you describe the God whom Jesus revealed at the wedding feast of Cana?

2) When have you seen in your life or in the life of someone close to you a change that could be compared to the changing of water into wine?

3) How would you express in your own words the change in the bread and wine that occurs in the Eucharist?

A Talk in the Night (John 3:1-21)

People's response to Jesus has not changed much in two thousand years. Then as now some ignored him; others rejected him. Some had a difficult time understanding and accepting what he taught. Others believed in him and found new life. It would be nice if at some point Jesus had spelled out in plain, simple and easily comprehensible language what that new life was all about. But, of course, he could not. Human language by its very nature can only suggest, hint at, give glimpses of the spiritual reality that comes from above. Those who take Jesus' words literally and in the context of what they have traditionally believed have great difficulty finding the spiritual reality behind his words.

Nicodemus had that problem. Like so many people after him, Nicodemus was thickheaded. He did not grasp that Jesus was talking about something new, something different from anything he knew. Obviously the new life Jesus empowers people to live is different from that which is nurtured in a mother's womb for nine months and sees daylight for the first time at birth. Nicodemus made the mistake of identifying the two when he asked Jesus, who had just told him about being born again, "How can anyone be born again after having grown old?" (3:4a). Jesus explained that his was a life not of flesh but of the Spirit that comes from above. Nicodemus could not see beyond physical life to a deeper, mysterious, divine type of life.

Nicodemus' vision of God and of how God works was too limited. He was trying to make God work in ways he could understand. Jesus rebuked him: "Are you a teacher of Israel, and yet you do not understand these things?" (3:10). Jesus was saying, "Nicodemus, you are not thinking straight. You have to hear what I am saying and interpret it in light of a deeper and wider view of God than you have from your past experience."

Obviously, Nicodemus knew of God's power manifested in the Exodus story and the consequent history of Israel. He knew of God's absolute power to work in wondrous ways and of God's overflowing love. But he was not able to see the connection between the way he understood these great realities and what Jesus was saying. He could not translate or transfer the knowledge he had of the past into the present situation, which was different from the Exodus and from the law miraculously delivered to the people.

Present-day readers of the Gospel often have to struggle to rethink their religious tradition, as Nicodemus had to do. They do not grasp that the Spirit is still active and may be calling them to see things differently than they see them as a result of their religious education. The Spirit may be calling them to broaden their vision of God, to rethink their image of Jesus, to change their view of Church. This call usually is not too clear and can be a bit frightening. It comes as a result of a changing world and of unexpected events such as an ecumenical council.

One of the most fundamental ideas we have to reconsider in the light of this Gospel is the way we see God. From the beginning of time people have striven to know God. They have carved images and drawn pictures to show what they think God is like. They have evolved profound mythologies to explain how God relates to the world and to human beings. They have developed mystical rites to help them leave the world of the senses and enter the world of the divine.

Jesus cut though all these human efforts by saying, "No one has ascended into heaven," implying that no one has seen God and therefore no one can know who God really is. But Jesus does not leave it at that. He immediately qualifies his statement and says that there is indeed one who can speak with authority about heavenly things, the Son of Man, who has come down from heaven and who will return to heaven. One and only one has seen God—Jesus himself. Then, as it were, with a brush of his hand he wipes away all philosophical, theological and mystical musings about God and pinpoints God's relationship to the world in two words: *love* and *life*. The God whom the Son has seen and reveals is a God of love, not of fear or power, a God who radiates light so that those who accept the light will have a new and different kind of life.

God's love for human beings defies understanding. It is totally gratuitous. Love is a reaching out to another that usually springs from seeing something attractive, desirable or helpful in the other. But there is nothing in human beings that is needed by or helpful to God. Even if all the people who have ever lived or ever will live stay in the dark, God is still God. The divine love is of another kind. It springs from God's goodness, from God's desire to share with others, to bring them into the light and give them eternal life. It is given without condition, without demanding a return of some kind.

Jesus said that this gift of love is eternal life. The gift is accepted by coming to the light, who is Jesus, and by doing works that can clearly be seen as being done in God. This life when accepted is eternal in two ways. First, it is a life that will continue to exist forever. Even though death seems to put an end to it, there is no end to it. Second, it is a life characterized by an abiding friendship with God.

The gift God offers is to be like God. One might ask,

27

"How can I be like God and still be me?" Perhaps a suitable comparison would be to the extensive remodeling we see when a shopping mall is remodeled or an old office building upgraded. Many things in these buildings are changed. Yet the basic structure remains the same. The remodelers have to work with the foundation, the existing walls and the supporting skeleton of the building. They may rearrange interior walls, but the outer walls remain even though they may be covered over. At times the structure may need to be retrofitted to make it earthquake-proof, but it remains substantially what it was.

In somewhat the same way the divine life builds on, reinforces, gives a new face to the natural life. Our temperament, talents and inclinations remain with us. They are the basic structure with which the Holy Spirit works, remodeling it slowly over the years. Our motives change. Our temperament may be modified and mellowed. Our talents may be put to different uses and our inclinations may be directed into other channels, but the unique self that the gracious and good God gave us at birth remains. Now, however, that one-of-a-kind individual we call "me" is "reborn" in God's likeness.

In another place John says that Jesus gives those who accept him the power to live as children of God (see John 1:12). This empowerment means that one can act in a positive, life-giving way in all circumstances. It means that we are not destined merely to react to forces outside of our control, but that we have the power to act in a positive way. It means that fears lingering from the past, active in the present or lurking in the future will not determine our life. It is the power to live in the present, doing the will of God, doing what we know to be right.

The power of love drives out all fear, gives witness to Jesus, shares, trusts, forgives and accepts the inevitable suffering that comes with these attitudes. Faith in Jesus as well as the life he shares overcomes a troubled heart and brings peace.

The Church celebrates the lives of many who were martyred for their faith. They were able to overcome the fear of pain and physical death and so to claim a deeper, eternal life with Christ. During the troubled times in Mexico when people were being persecuted for their faith, those being executed by a firing squad were often heard to cry out, *"Viva Christo Rey!"* ("Long live Christ the King!"). In the moment of their death they turned fearlessly to the deeper reality of God's presence, love and promise of eternal life.

Nicodemus is a good example of being born again. From later incidents we can deduce how the new life, the light Jesus speaks of, transformed a human life. At first Nicodemus did not comprehend what Jesus was talking about. Most likely he went away puzzled and still asking questions in his head. We hear no more of him for three years. Then we see the same man with the same position in life, yet different. When the chief priests and Pharisees want to have Jesus arrested, Nicodemus speaks up for him: "Our law does not judge people without first giving them a hearing to find out what they are doing, does it?" (7:51).

Nicodemus suffered the ridicule of his peers just for wanting justice done. The road to friendship with Jesus is paved with crises that often ask us to stand against current and popular trends in society. We do not know how, when or if Nicodemus ever became a professed disciple of Jesus. Nevertheless, when the apostles and the other disciples were in hiding after the crucifixion, he was brave enough to go openly with Joseph of Arimathea to bury Jesus (see John 19:39-40). More than that, he brought enough myrrh and aloes to embalm a king rather than the minimal amount needed for an ordinary burial, especially that of a common criminal. The meaning of Jesus' talk that first night evidently sank in. At some point Nicodemus believed, received new life and become courageous enough to act in the face of scorn and ridicule.

FOR REFLECTION

1) *The Spirit is always moving the Church in unexpected ways. How many of these unexpected and unaccustomed directions the Church has taken in the past decades can you name?*

2) *What does the story of Nicodemus suggest to you about the nature of the God Jesus revealed?*

3) *In your own words, share how you have experienced the power of new life in your life and how your faith has led you to act in a courageous way.*

Chapter Three

The Hour Is Now

S TORIES ARE A WONDERFUL TEACHING MEDIUM. They offer so many levels of understanding that hearers can find many different messages in them. These messages are not always those intended by the author.

John had a very definite purpose in placing each incident in the life of Jesus where he did. He was highlighting the power and person of Jesus as well as showing the growing opposition to him. Scholars write very convincingly about why a certain incident is in a certain place and how it contributes to the overall purpose of John's Gospel.

Nevertheless, preachers, spiritual directors and ordinary readers often find other meanings in these stories. John may or may not have been conscious of such secondary meanings, but they still can foster the growth of the life Jesus shares with us because the Spirit is present to open our hearts to ever deeper meanings of the Scriptures.

Three incidents in the first part of the Gospel, Jesus' meeting with the woman at the well, his cure of the man born blind and the raising of Lazarus, show that the fears engendered by the past, by the present or by the future come under control when Jesus enters our life. So crucial are these three stories to faith in Jesus that they are the Gospels assigned to the final weeks of Lent in parishes where catechumens are journeying toward Easter Baptism.

Fear is a strong word that covers many lesser emotions. For example, fear of the past may mean that we are worried about what might happen to us if our past is revealed. Even when we are not afraid of revelation, we still may feel shame, guilt or regret about a past action. At times these are good sentiments to have, but if we constantly dwell on the event or on the shame we felt and do not learn from it, then that fear is debilitating; it hinders God's action in our lives. In the story of the woman at the well the fear of rejection, of being harshly judged because of her past life and her present situation, is dismissed by the actions of Jesus.

Fear of the present in its obvious form is a reaction to a threat to one's health, life or welfare. This is nature's way of warning us and preparing us to face the danger. At times it can cause us to dwell on the perceived threat to such a degree that we ignore the helps that are available to us. Or it can turn us in on ourselves to such a degree that we may not be able to distinguish between a mere possibility of danger and a real threat to our well-being. Feelings associated with this kind of fear are stress, worry, concern, uncertainty and undue anxiety. In the story of the man born blind the fear arising from a real threat, namely a rebuff by the rabbis and ejection from the synagogue, is overcome.

Finally, the fear of the future may have a real basis in uncertainty about one's life, health or future welfare. If that is the case, trust in Jesus does not wipe out the fear nor does it assure one that everything will work out as one would have it. It does give one the ability to work through the situation in the best way one can with the assurance that God is near. For example, when Martha mourns the death of her brother, Lazarus, we can read in her words concern about what will happen to her and her sister now that Lazarus is gone. Jesus asks her to trust him, and then works a miracle to show that her trust is not misplaced.

These three stories indicate that the new life in Jesus is a life of hope and confidence, a life that brings peace and overcomes fear. It is a life to be lived in the present, not shackled to the past or anxious about the future.

'Can You Give a Thirsty Man a Drink?'
(John 4:4-26)

Imagine going into a laundromat and being asked by a complete stranger for a cup of detergent to wash his clothes. Push your imagination a little further and hear what you might say to him and what he might say to you. He seems nice enough, but you have been warned not to be friendly to strangers. Soon he is offering you an unlimited supply of free detergent. Would you not be suspicious of a man making such an offer when he did not have enough to wash his own clothes? Would not your suspicion grow if he promised that he could arrange it that you would never have to go to the laundromat again? Imagine your astonishment if he began to tell you a nasty little secret about yourself that no stranger could possibly know. How quickly would you move away from him, look around for help or call the police? Would you be willing to hear him out?

Long ago a woman had just such an encounter at a well in Samaria. She had gone to draw water some distance from her home. It was a daily chore but that did not make it any easier. She had to walk to the well, drop the bucket, pull it up by a rope, pour it into a jar, put the jar on her head and carry it home. On some days she would have to make more than one trip.

Then one noon a stranger asked her for a drink. She gave it to him. He in turn offered her living water. Now she was surprised, because she knew living water came from a spring—fresh, clear and easy to scoop into a jar.

He told her that she had misunderstood him. The living water he offered was refreshing and never-ending, but of a different kind than the water in her jar. They got into a bit of a theological discussion about the proper place to offer sacrifice. Was it Jerusalem or Gerizim? Finally, he got a bit more personal and asked her to go fetch her husband. She replied that she had none. He agreed and told her that she had had five and that the man she was now living with was not her husband.

Her reaction was interesting. It was not the denial or indignation we might expect when out of the blue a stranger accused her of adultery. She heard something beyond the spoken words. She saw a prophet behind the face of the weary, dusty stranger. Then she heard the most amazing assertion: He indeed was a prophet. More than that, he was *the* prophet whom both Jews and Samaritans had been hoping for.

It is impossible to spell out in literal language what Jesus meant by inexhaustible living water. The phrase is symbolic; it conceals more than it reveals because the reality is beyond human comprehension. Even when symbols such as this one are analyzed and interpreted, the underlying reality is not seen clearly in all its richness. We have to be satisfied with saying, "It is something like this."

Water is a vivid symbol of the life that comes from the infinite power of God-within because it is an essential element in the makeup of physical life. Four-fifths of the earth's surface is covered with water; out of the waters of the oceans all forms of fish, bird and animal life have emerged. Human beings spend the first nine months of their existence immersed in the water of their mother's womb. Even after birth, well over seventy-five percent of the human body is composed of water.

Not only is water fundamental to all life, in a very real sense it also gives life. When there is no water, living things die. When there is water, and especially where it is abundant, life is not only sustained but made to flourish.

In very real ways the life Jesus offers is like water because it is generative, nourishing, abundant, fruitful and easily available. At the same time this new life is different from water because it is not physical. It cannot be seen, felt, smelled or even heard. It is a new state of being. We are not sure exactly how it transforms the physical life we have from our natural birth. It can never be explained in a way our logical, concrete, earthbound intellect desires. Symbols need to be grasped with imagination, with faith and trust, with love. Only then do they make the kind of sense that leads to eternal life.

The living water—the life—Jesus offers is the ability to see the world through his eyes. It is the ability to interpret and judge people and events as God does. For example, when Jesus looked at the woman with the water jar, he saw more than the features of her face, the color and style of her clothes. He saw beyond what his culture had conditioned him to see in women and in Samaritans. He saw a person who suffered from many forms of rejection.

A female, she was considered inferior to men and treated as the chattel of her father or husband. She belonged to an ethnic and religious group rejected by the larger and more powerful religious establishment. The Jews considered the Samaritans one step above Gentiles—half-pagan heretics and religious outcasts. Their attitude must have been akin to that of Muslim fundamentalists toward Muslims open to Western culture or to that of biblical fundamentalists who believe that those who do not think as they do are doomed. Finally, she must have experienced some rejection from the people in her own community. The fact that she came to the well alone at noon, the hottest and least desirable time of the day, suggests she was not welcome when the women usually gathered to draw water and talk. All in all, she was the most unlikely person to be the first recipient of Jesus' revelation that he was the Messiah.

Jesus saw in the woman an undiscovered greatness that neither she nor others saw because of the barriers that blocked their vision. They saw the externals of her life and all its complications. Jesus looked at her in a new way. He saw her with the eyes of love. He saw her with the eyes of God. In the kindly and understanding way Jesus related to this woman standing at the well, we catch a glimpse of the way God relates to people of either gender, of any ethnic background or faith. Jesus looked at her with an understanding heart, the heart of God. From that view flowed his attitude of openness, respect and attention.

By the way he spoke to her he swept away all the barriers of culture and personal history that separated him from her. It did not now matter that she was a Samaritan and a woman. The age-old taboo against a man speaking to a woman in public did not faze him a bit. Her religious beliefs, the result of hundreds of years of religious differences between Samaritans and Jews, did not keep him from offering her the waters of life. The fact that she had been living an irregular life-style did not preclude him from approaching her and asking for a favor. The living waters he had come to share did not depend on the past or on any social convention. They were for the present.

By sweeping away the barriers from the past, Jesus freed the woman from the fear that would have kept her at a distance from him. He freed her from her prejudices against the Jews so she could accept him as the Messiah. He freed her from her fear of rejection so she was able to acknowledge her life-style to the people of her town and by this openness motivate them to go out and hear what Jesus had to offer. Personal witness such as hers has great power to open others to a new vision of life and to move them. It often opens new vistas to the people who hear it. For instance, the testimonies of people in Alcoholics Anonymous often bring hope and help to others who desire to live a new and sober life-style.

The story of the woman at the well demonstrates that her past was not wiped out or ignored but that it became the occasion for her to find the Messiah. We can only speculate what her reaction would have been if she had been bound by the conventions of the past about not dealing with men or Jews, or if the guilt and hurt of her past life had blocked her from recognizing Jesus as a prophet. She did not ignore the conventions. She asked why a Jew was asking her for a favor. She did not ignore her past life or blame the men involved, but admitted it, simply stating the facts. Neither did Jesus ignore past religious differences or her life-style. He acknowledged them, but moved beyond them. They ceased to matter when an offer of living water, of a new way of seeing life, of a different kind of life was being made.

Interpreting the present only in terms of what one has experienced in the past blocks one's ability to see the opportunity for the better and richer life offered in the present. This past can be idealized. It can be seen as a golden age that once was. It can be a longing for good and helpful experiences and practices that once were growth-giving, but that now seem to have lost their attraction and power. Thus the present can be doomed to frustration if one sees it merely as an opportunity to repeat a good experience without recognizing that the present is unique and presents new and unique opportunities. The past is never repeatable.

Human beings tend to fantasize about the "good old days" when everything was perfect and life was a breeze. Circumstances that cannot be duplicated may make life seem to have been better in the past. The present, even a very painful present, presents new opportunities to grow and become better human beings if one does not constantly compare the present situation to the past, but looks at it from a different viewpoint.

A woman once came to a counselor with marriage problems. In the course of the session she complained that her husband was cold and unresponsive and was never, in all their years of marriage, able to respond to her true emotional needs.

The counselor listened attentively and began to see that the woman's ideal of a perfect mate had come from a high school romance some twenty years before. She had been in love with a young man in her senior year and hoped to marry him. The relationship ended disastrously when the young man took up with another girl.

Through counseling the woman gained insight into the fact that she had been comparing her husband to this previous heartthrob. The man she was married to was no match for the fantasy she had spun around her old flame. Her anger at her husband was covering up the pain of her loss. This effort to recapture the romantic feelings of the past was poisoning her present attitude toward her husband. No way could he live up to the ideal picture she had created in her mind.

As she began to realize that her husband was not the high school senior she had once loved, that he was not able to live up to her idealized expectations, a new peace began to grow in her. For the first time she began to see her husband as the good and loving person he was. She began to allow herself to experience the love that was in his heart. Gradually things began to change for the better in her life and in her marriage. A couple of years after her counseling sessions had ended, she met her old flame at a high school reunion. She was shocked to find that he was a middle-aged man, balding, bulging and extremely boring. Sadly she realized that she had wasted the early years of her marriage comparing her husband to the "perfect spouse" who existed only in her head and who would have never brought her the happiness she was now experiencing in her marriage.

In a similar way the vision of life that Jesus offers as living water helps us see the mistakes and the fantasies of the past for what they are and helps us find in the present the way to a fulfilling life in God.

The past can also hold unpleasant memories that make it impossible to see that the present situation is different and life-giving. Accepting the living water Jesus offers involves handing our past sins, mistakes, faults, social conventions, even rigid religious beliefs or practices to him on open hands and letting them go. If we brood over our past mistakes, if we hang on to the resentment, the bitterness, the anger, the frustration, the depression that come from past broken relationships and failures, if we hold old religious practices and even beliefs unchangeable, we are crippled in our ability to appreciate the love and goodness God exhibits right here and now. We close our eyes to the living water Jesus offers. The past is often one of the main reasons people refuse to accept the gift Jesus offers. They fear what they might lose if they do so and prefer to hang on to what they saw as good in the past.

An old lady refused to cooperate with the nurses at a medical center. She screamed at anyone who touched her. To treat the sores on her body, the nurses removed her clothes and washed her, but she kept her fists so tightly closed that the nurses could not pry them open. Finally, two male nurses pried her fingers apart. In each palm was a small coin. She clung to these coins as though she would lose herself if she lost them. She was afraid that if they were taken from her, she would have nothing more, be nothing more. Letting go of those coins was painful, yet she needed to let go of them before any treatment could begin.

In some way people who cling to the past are like that old woman. They want to hold fast to what is familiar even though they may not be proud of it. They find it safer to hang on to the few coins in their hands than to put their trust in the Lord.

Putting aside the fears from the past and accepting the gift of living water is not enough, however, to ensure that one will never thirst again and that the living water will become a spring welling up to eternal life. It is also necessary to cooperate with the gift of life and to share it with others.

Take as an example the waters that flow into the Sea of Galilee and those that flow into the Dead Sea. The Sea of Galilee receives water from the surrounding mountains and allows it to overflow into the Jordan River, which in turn beings life to the valley below. The Jordan empties into the Dead Sea, which has no outlet. It holds all the water that flows into it. Because there is no way for the water to circulate or flow out, it becomes very salty; no life can live in it. Unable to release the water given to it by the Jordan, it cannot give life.

The same is true of the life and gifts God gives us. If we do not share them with others, they will dry up and die. As the Bob Dylan song says, the person who is "not busy being born is busy dying."

We do not know what the Samaritan woman did about her marital situation, but we do know how she sought to share with others the life that had been given her. We read that when the disciples returned from buying groceries, "the woman left her water jar and went back to the city. She said to the people, 'Come and see a man who told me everything I have ever done! He cannot be the Messiah, can he?' " (4:28-29).

She had come to draw water. Yet she set aside the task at hand in order to go and tell people who did not think highly of her what had happened to her and the conclusion she had drawn from the incident. When a person begins to realize how profoundly different is the life Jesus offers, that person cannot keep it locked in his or her heart. By its very nature the living water has to be shared. It is water intended for all, available to all and free to all.

The opportunity to share the living water presents itself today in ways just as unexpected as the meeting of Jesus with the woman at the well. A couple who had been born Jewish but who admitted that they were more agnostics than believers moved into a new neighborhood some years ago. Several of the neighbors pitched in to help him fix a porch. When it was completed the couple hosted a barbecue to thank them. The day after the barbecue, one of the neighbors asked if the couple would be offended if she talked to them about God. They said that they did not mind and invited her to come for morning coffee.

Practically every day for six months she had coffee with them and shared with them her enthusiasm about God. She never argued. She respected their doubts and questions. She encouraged them to talk with the local rabbi. When they finally said that they thought they believed in God, she asked if they minded if she told them about Jesus. After another six months of morning coffee talks they accepted Jesus as the Messiah and were baptized.

New life is not embraced without a struggle; neither

does it mature and grow without one. The various indications of the nature of new life reveal where the struggle lies. It is not easy to overcome the taboos and prejudices of our society and see people with the heart instead of merely with the eyes or the mind. It is not easy to open a conversation about faith, especially with someone who is not of our faith. It is not easy to understand who Jesus is or what new life means. It is not easy to set down our jar, the daily tasks at hand, and go to share with others either by word or by our actions our joy in new life. The way we deal with these struggles either helps new life grow, allowing the water to flow freely, or it weakens it, damming the waters of life.

FOR REFLECTION

1) *Think of someone who struck up a conversation with you or whom you met for the first time. What did you see with your eyes? What did your mind and feelings tell you about the person's race, culture, religion, social standing? What did you eventually see in that person beyond what your mind and eye saw?*

2) *What adjectives do you associate with living water and what do they suggest to you about the life Jesus offers?*

3) *What does this story suggest to you about the way God relates to people?*

4) *What are some of the fears from the past that hinder you from accepting the new life Jesus offers?*

5) *Share a story of a person being brought to Christ by the love and sharing of another person.*

The Light of the World (John 9:1-41)

On January 17, 1994, an earthquake struck Los Angeles

41

at 4:31 A.M. Buildings rocked and slid off their foundations. Walls collapsed. Chimneys fell. Books and glass crashed to the floor. People scrambled out of bed, groped for flashlights and fled their homes.

Afterward, many commented on feeling blind—not because their eyes were injured but because not even a tiny night light glowed. The entire city was dark. No window lights, no yard lights, no street lights cast a glow. The next sensation many people felt was one of wonderment. They looked up and saw the stars in the sky. On most nights city lights and smog obscure all but the brightest stars. That night thousands of stars could be seen clearly. A third sensation was relief as sections of the city gradually lit up and electricity came back to their homes.

John frequently uses the powerful images of light and darkness, sight and blindness. For him seeing is much more than physical sight; light is much more than the glow of a fire or of a lamp. Sight and light suggest understanding, heeding, being conscious of a profound truth. Yet seeing is more than grasping the truth with the mind. It is discerning and appropriating the hidden reality of God in a given situation. Jesus told Nicodemus that "all who do evil hate the light and do not come to the light, so that their deeds might not be exposed. But those who do what is true come to the light, so that it may be clearly seen that their deeds have been done in God" (3:20-21). Before he cured the man born blind Jesus clearly explained what and who that light was: "As long as I am in the world, I am the light of the world" (9:5).

The story of the beggar born blind indicates the ways people are drawn to and accept the light and the ways they resist the light and prefer to live and work in the darkness. The blind man did not ask to be cured. Jesus saw that he was blind, walked up to him, mixed spittle with dirt, rubbed the mess on the sightless eyes and told the man to go and wash. The blind man had no reason to believe that washing mud from his eyes would help him in any way. Yet he did not question Jesus' directive. He did not ask why the mud was

42

put on his eyes or why Jesus did not merely say the word and cure him. He did what Jesus told him to do in spite of what his thoughts or feelings may have been. He went to the pool and washed his eyes.

As the water took away the mud, he began to see. Grateful, he went back to the pool area looking for Jesus, but Jesus was gone.

Although sight had come to his eyes, he still had a long way to go before he was spiritually enlightened. He had to face the questions of his neighbors, the ridicule of the Pharisees, his parents' lack of support and even expulsion from the synagogue. Through all of this he had to trust his interpretation of his experience. When he did finally meet Jesus, all he could do was cry out, "I do believe" and worship.

Today we have no more reason than the blind beggar had to believe that Jesus makes a difference in our lives, that he will give us light and sight. Often the things he tells us to do make little sense: Revenge seems better than forgiving an enemy; riches surely are better than selling all and following him; lying or at least skirting the truth is more advantageous than saying yes when we mean yes and no when we mean no. Two attitudes are essential: Trust in the words of Jesus even when they seem to make little sense; courage to stand by one's conviction that Jesus is from God.

Jesus opened the eyes of the beggar so the man could see Jesus as one sent by God. But he also opened the eyes of the disciples so they could put aside their notion that illness was a punishment from God and achieve a clearer vision of how God works. The story suggests that most people have too small a picture of God and need to broaden their vision.

Some people still think that misfortune or illness are punishments from God for their sins. They do not trust Jesus' words that God is a loving God who wills only good for people. They cannot live with the seeming contradiction that God is a loving God and at the same time a God of freedom. They argue that a God who loves would not allow the actions of others to bring misery to the world and would prevent natural disasters like the Los Angeles earthquake.

The God of the Old Testament, who is the same God Jesus reveals, gives freedom. God is gracious enough to allow people to walk toward the light or to walk away from it, to choose to live in the light or to choose to work in the darkness, free to help others or to do hurtful things to themselves and to others. This is not a meddling God who alters the course of nature when earthquakes, droughts and floods bring devastation. The ways of this God are beyond human comprehension because in some mysterious way they bring love, freedom and suffering together.

This story makes clear that we have to look for the cause of suffering in a source other than God. The Gospel clearly shows that Jesus never visited punishment on anyone who ignored him or even hated him. It is easy to see that much suffering is caused by nature, either in its most obvious forms of storm and earthquake or in the tiny form of a mutant gene or a virus.

It is not as easy to trace the cause of much individual suffering, of people's inhumanity to people, of struggles for power and for wealth. Often it is very difficult to accept that suffering in one's life is the result of living and working in a self-chosen darkness that exacts a natural toll. We have only to look at the effects of drug or alcohol abuse to see that the violation of the way God has created us has its own serious consequences without any divine intervention.

The story also illustrates how some people refused the enlightenment Jesus offered, preferring to remain in the darkness. The Pharisees caught the drift of Jesus' words when they asked, "Surely, we are not blind, are we?" (9:40b). Jesus assured them that they were indeed blind because they felt sure that they were able to see the truth in all situations when the truth actually was different from their set view. The physical blindness of the man and the mental blindness of the Pharisees are symbolic of how the present, as well as the past, can block one from the freeing action of Jesus.

Spiritual blindness comes from thinking that because

of my education, my status in the community, my experience, my understanding of my faith I always know exactly the reality of a given situation and God's will for those involved. Often, therefore, our words are moralizing sermons full of *should, ought* and *have to*. For example, my expectations of how God works can blind me to the good in people I think are sinners. It can also blind me to God's coming in completely unexpected ways, as Jesus came to the blind beggar.

Spiritual blindness is also the result of a vision of life restricted to the physical and to the present. Because the spiritual cannot be seen, felt, touched, smelled or heard, it is ignored or denied. Consumerism, the desire for pleasure here and now, distrust of all authority—all these restrict one's vision of life to the physical and the immediate and contribute to blinding people to the hidden action of God in the present.

It is interesting that not once in the story of the blind man did anyone seem to notice (much less be moved by the fact) that the man received physical sight from Jesus. The Pharisees, wedded to their hatred of Jesus, were blind to the new reality and the gift of light that was being offered to them.

Perhaps their attitude is the greatest cause of spiritual blindness: a closed mind that rejects any idea but its own or that tries to force reality into the mold it wants. Those who think they fully understand what is going on and refuse to look at things from a different point of view can easily overlook the deeper spiritual challenge being presented by God. We only have to look at the way the Church in the sixteenth century reacted to Copernicus, who said that the earth was not the center of the universe. Contrary to what people's eyes told them, he insisted that the earth rotated around the sun and not the sun around the earth. He was saying that things were not as they seemed. This new idea was very threatening to the way theologians explained the world at that time. As a result Copernicus was actively persecuted as a troublemaker and a heretic.

With the same mindset, the Pharisees thought they understood the situation of the blind man and refused to give credence to his explanation of what had happened. They freely chose to be blind to any explanation but their own for his cure. They could not see that this cure was calling them to a new understanding of God and to faith in Jesus. They could not accept something radically different from their explanation of why the man was blind and of how he was cured because they would have to give up their old system of interpreting life along with their power to dominate the thinking of others.

FOR REFLECTION

1) *When have you trusted your experience even though others doubted or denied it?*

2) *What in the story of the man born blind encourages you to trust in Jesus even though his words do not always seem to make sense to you?*

3) *How do you reconcile in your own mind that the God Jesus reveals as loving and caring is also a God who apparently allows bad things to happen to good people?*

4) *If at times you have felt that God was punishing you for some past sin, how did you handle that thought?*

'Unbind Him and Let Him Go!' (John 11:1-44)

Time and fear are great obstacles to accepting, living and deepening the life Jesus has given us in Baptism. Fear that our past will be held against us or that it will be made known blocks us from living fully in the present. Jesus negated this fear of the past when he met the woman at the well and empowered her to see beyond her prejudices to the gift being offered in the present.

Fear that we may have to change our present way of seeing life and perhaps do something that makes little or no sense to us blocks us from appreciating the opportunities offered to us here and now. When Jesus gave the man born blind instructions to wash the mud from his eyes, he opened a whole new world to him and empowered him to take a stand against the forces that would deny his experience.

Fear of the future, of the unknown, of that which we cannot control causes us to become overly anxious, to do foolish things, even to lose hope. This is cleverly illustrated in a story about a man so worried about the future that he actually brought about the catastrophe he feared. As W. Somerset Maugham tells us in his play, *Sheppy*:

> There was a merchant in Baghdad who sent his servant to buy provisions. In a little while the servant came back, white and trembling, and said, "Master, just now when I was in the marketplace I was jostled by a woman in the crowd and when I turned around I saw it was Death that jostled me. She looked at me and made a threatening gesture; now lend me your horse, and I will ride away from this city and avoid my fate. I will go to Samarra and there Death will not find me."
> The merchant lent him his horse, and the servant mounted it, and he dug his spurs in its flanks and as fast as the horse could gallop he raced off to Samarra. Later that day the merchant went down to the market-place and he saw Death standing in the crowd. He went up to Death and asked, "Why did you make a threatening gesture to my servant when you saw him this morning?" Said Death, "It was only a start of surprise. I was astonished to see your servant in Baghdad for I have an appointment with him tonight in Samarra!"

Anyone who has picked up a phone and heard a call to come quickly because a friend or family member was close to death can appreciate the feeling Jesus must have had when a messenger arrived at the door of the house where he was staying with the news that his friend Lazarus was deathly sick. But, instead of packing up and going to Bethany, Jesus loitered for two more days before saying that Lazarus was asleep and it was time to go.

Of course, the disciples wanted to know what the hurry was now that Lazarus seemed to be getting better. Then Jesus spoke plainly: "Lazarus has died." He gave the reason for tarrying: "For your sake I am glad I was not there, so that you may believe" (11:15b). He was going to give them another sign to confirm their faith in him. It would seem that by this time their faith should have been strong, but still they needed signs of his power. It is interesting that when people came and asked for signs Jesus refused to give them, but that he spontaneously gave unexpected and different kinds of signs to his disciples to confirm the faith they had in him.

When Jesus had finally arrived at Bethany, Martha chided him. She knew that he could have cured her brother: "Lord, if you had been here, my brother would not have died" (11:21b). Her brother's death confronted Martha with an event that causes hearts to break, releasing waves of fear, anger, regret and hopelessness.

In response, Jesus addressed the reality of her grief and offered hope: "I am the resurrection and the life. Those who believe in me, even though they die, will live, and everyone who lives and believes in me will never die. Do you believe this?" (11:25b-26). The fear that we will never again see those whom we love after death can only be overcome by disbelieving the testimony of our eyes and seeing death through the eyes of Jesus—seeing it as God does, as a transition to a new life.

The new life Jesus implanted in us at Baptism will not be issued to us when we enter the pearly gates. It begins in the here and now and continues into eternity. The tenor of that life is set by what we do each day. Death is merely the end of the physical life we know. Our life in Jesus will continue in another form. The raising of Lazarus, like all signs, is inadequate to convey the richness and the fullness of the reality of this life. Eternal life exceeds beyond all measure the physical life we now possess. It exceeds anything our imagination can conceive. Yet it exists and is ours when we make the ultimate act of faith and accept Jesus not merely as a teacher and a good man, but as "the resurrection and the life" in face of the physical fact of death.

Jesus wept when he faced the tomb. He was not afraid to show his emotions. He felt the loss of his friend, just as anyone does. His tears reflect the face of a compassionate God who, as it were, cries with us in our misfortune. But Jesus' action in calling Lazarus to come out of the tomb also shows that God has power even over death, the final and greatest evil, the source of the ultimate fear.

Jesus tested the faith of the bystanders by asking them to roll away the stone. They could see no good reason for this. The man had been dead for four days. He would not be anything to look at and the stench would be powerful. Faith can call us to do seemingly crazy things. When the stone was rolled back, Lazarus did come out alive.

"Unbind him and let him go," Jesus said (11:44c). These words were an obvious practical directive because Lazarus was wrapped like a mummy. Yet we can see a deeper or symbolic meaning in them. The life Jesus shares with believers frees them and lets them go. From what are they freed? They are freed from the wrappings and restraints of their previous life, of their sins, of their fears about the present and the future and of their limited way of seeing reality.

It is interesting that Jesus himself did not step forward and unwrap Lazarus. He told the bystanders to do so. Jesus indeed gives life, but we need a community to help free us so that we can live that life. We need a community that frees us from the bonds of past expectations and failures, that helps us to walk in freedom and supports us in our efforts to live our new life.

In a very real sense, people who die to one way of life

in order to embrace a new and better way need to find new friends to help them along, to help free them from the past. This is clearly borne out when we look at the prison system. Released prisoners who have every intention of going straight will most likely fall into crime again if they do not find new friends to help them lead a new kind of life. Thus, those who accept Jesus in faith or those whose indifferent faith catches fire need to find a community of like-minded believers to reinforce and strengthen their faith. Then they in turn can help untie others bound by fear of the past, present or future so that they too can bring light into the darkness of the present age.

FOR REFLECTION

1) *When someone has died, what fears about the future have you experienced?*

2) *What questions have you asked or wanted to ask of God when someone close to you has died?*

3) *What kind of freedom does believing that Jesus actually has overcome death give you in the present?*

4) *What community helps to untie you and helps you to love in the present?*

Chapter Four

The Freedom to Choose

THE GOD WHO REVEALS HIMSELF in Jesus defies people's image of the divine. One characteristic that all people have attributed to their gods has been power—power to crush enemies, power over the forces of nature, power over the lives of human beings. In the sign stories John shows Jesus exercising remarkable power over nature by curing the sick, walking on the water and raising the dead to life. John shows him exercising the power of God to forgive sins, but at the same time he shows Jesus as seemingly powerless over the thoughts and actions of people. Jesus did not tinker with their minds so that they had to believe in him. He just went about doing his Father's business and allowed people the freedom to believe or not to believe. To the skepticism, suspicion and misunderstanding of those who did not accept him, he responded in language that was not always easy to understand and let it go at that.

Even as criticism and opposition mounted, Jesus always allowed people to feel, to think and to act as they pleased. In Jesus' encounters with his enemies we see a loving God who gives the beloved, in this case his enemies, the most precious gift of all: the gift of freedom to choose.

'Not on the Sabbath!' (John 5:1-47)

People look for a miraculous cure when doctors and medicine fail them. The Jews were no exception. By our standards the medical profession of that day was primitive. The only recourse for many of the sick was to seek divine help.

There was a pool in Jerusalem that was believed to have curative powers for the first person who stepped into it after the waters had been stirred by some unseen force. Tradition attributed the movement of the water to an angel's descent from heaven. Scientists today think the movement may have been caused by a bubbling up of the spring that fed the pool.

One poor man had been ill for thirty-eight years. He waited by the pool expectantly, but no one would help him get to the head of the line. Jesus spotted the man, asked him if he wanted to get well and told him to take up his mat and walk—which he did. On the face of it this was but another manifestation of Jesus' concern for one who was suffering.

But there was more to it than that. Jesus was setting the stage for a powerful assertion of his power as the giver of life and of his special relationship with the Father. He did not have to cure that man on the sabbath. Waiting one more day after thirty-eight years of being crippled would not have been a great inconvenience for him. Jesus could have waited another twenty-four hours and not violated the prohibition against working—curing—on the sabbath. He did not wait. He acted. It is difficult to imagine that Jesus did not foresee that the cure would cause an angry reaction from those who already were not friendly to him, those whom John calls "the Jews."

In John's Gospel "the Jews" are not very nice people. He uses that term not to refer to all the children of Israel but to identify a small group of people who were enemies of Jesus. This Gospel was written in its final form sometime between A.D 90 and 100. At the time Christians were being persecuted by the Romans. In A.D. 85, the Jewish leaders passed a law that Jewish Christians would no longer be protected by the synagogue. This meant that they could not escape the Roman law by claiming to be Jews, who were allowed to follow their belief in one God who was not Caesar. This action may have heightened John's feelings of anger against the Jewish leaders whom he saw as enemies of Christ.

The evangelist uses the word *Jews* in much the same way as Russians and Americans called each other capitalists or communists during the Cold War. Ordinary Russian people would say that it was not the American *people* who were their enemy (in fact, they were friendly to American tourists), but the capitalistic bankers and leaders of the government, who wanted to wipe them out. Similarly, Americans would say that it was not Russian workers who were the enemy, but the leaders of the government and a relatively small number of dedicated party members who were plotting to destroy our way of life.

The sordid history of the persecution of the Jewish people by Christians over the centuries makes us wish that John and the other Gospel writers would have been less generic and more specific in naming the enemies of Jesus. They did not have the prophetic foresight to see how their words would be misinterpreted and distorted by later generations for less than noble reasons.

In any case, those who were unfriendly to Jesus were always looking for an occasion to trip him up. In this cure they felt that they had a perfect case to show that he was not really a good Jew. He did on the sabbath what could have easily been postponed to the next day. When his enemies pointed this out to Jesus, he asserted that he certainly had the right to work on the sabbath because God, his Father, works on the seventh day as well as on the other six days.

In spite of what the Book of Genesis says about God resting on the seventh day, the rabbis recognized that all of God's activity could not cease one day a week. God still had to keep the world in existence. He had to give life because children were born on that day; he had to take it away because people died on the seventh day as well as on the other six. Neither did God suspend his judgment on human behavior on that day.

Jesus asserts that, like the Father, he too works on the sabbath. Like the Father, he gives life—in this case eternal life. He too has the power to judge. This was a staggering claim for a man from the countryside to make. His enemies correctly understood his claim to be equal to God. For a people who had struggled and suffered for generations because they believed that there was only one God, this was the most heinous of blasphemies. Therefore they decided to kill him. Jesus showed how much he was like his Father by not using his power to stop them, by not miraculously opening their minds and hearts to his words, by not destroying them. He left them free.

Incomprehension of Jesus' words did not cease with those whom John calls "the Jews." It plagued the Church for many centuries after the Resurrection. In the first six centuries people suggested all sorts of explanations of how one person could be true God and true man. Some said that God adopted Jesus as his Son. Others said that the Son of God was created from a substance other than that of the Father. Still others said that Jesus' human nature ceased to exist when it was assumed by the divine nature of God, and so on. The early Councils of the Church condemned these various heresies, but that did not end the controversies. The divisions caused by them still exist as a barrier to the union of Christian Churches.

Even though there are no longer bitter theological arguments about whether or not Jesus is both true God and true man, people still demonstrate the same incomprehension as the Jews of Jesus' time. Some people who profess to be Christian deny or question the divinity of Jesus. They accept his humanity, but religious polls show that many, even Catholics, see him merely as a great teacher and a great humanitarian and doubt or deny his true divinity. Other Christians in effect deny his humanity because they see him only as God.

Jesus offered his opponents four reasons for accepting him, none of which they accepted. The first was the testimony of John the Baptist. The second was the works he did among them. The third was the interior voice of God speaking to them. The fourth was the Scriptures. These are the same reasons offered to us. The evangelists, the great theologians, the persuasive preachers can lay out compelling arguments to prove Jesus' claim. But accepting him, not ignoring him or rejecting him, is a matter of faith, of plunging into the dark, of choosing belief over denial.

We also are being offered a choice: Here stands Jesus! Accept or reject his claim to be equal to the Father. You are free to do either; God will not force you to believe. If you accept him you will honor the Father; you will pass from death to life, and if you have tried to live that new life, you will rise to eternal life. If you reject him, you do not honor the Father who sent him and you will rise to condemnation.

FOR REFLECTION

1) *How do you feel about letting people be free to choose their own life-style, religion, profession, etc.?*

2) *What does Jesus' action suggest to you about God's activity in the world today?*

3) *Why would you say that a person is failing to live the life Christ offers if he or she is anti-Semitic?*

4) *Share an incident of something you did because you thought it was the right thing to do even though others discouraged you or disagreed with you.*

5) *What are the most compelling reasons you have for accepting Jesus as the Son of God sent into the world?*

Chapter Five
God Lives Among Us

A CHARMING STORY HELPS us understand what Jesus was talking about when he used five barley loaves and two fish to feed several thousand people:

> At the beginning of creation God assembled all the angels before him and said, "My favorite creatures, human beings, are so fearful. They think that I am not present to them and that I do not love them. I want to become a part of creation so that when they experience this part they will know that I am with them and that I love them. What can I become?"
>
> One of the angels suggested that God become the sun so that when people experienced its light and heat they would know that he was with them and loved them.
>
> God responded, "But you know that it is dark half the time on earth. At those dark times people will not see me and will doubt that I am with them and love them. Does anyone else have an idea?"
>
> Another angel spoke up, "God, why don't you become the wind? When humans feel the wind blowing and are refreshed by its gentle touch they will know that you are with them and that you love them."
>
> "Not bad," said God, "but you know that there are great periods of calm on the earth when there is no breeze at all. During these times human beings will doubt that I am with them and love them."
>
> Another angel called out, "Lord, become water! When humans see water and feel its refreshing taste in their mouths they will think of you and of your love for them."

Again God said, "Not bad!" but after a moment's reflection added, "There are great deserts on the earth and when people are in these dry places they will surely doubt my presence and my love for them. Can anyone else think of what I might become so that humans will know that I am always present and that my love is everlasting?"

After a long time one of the smallest angels spoke out, "God, why don't you become bread? For when humans eat bread they will know that you are present and that you love them.

"Brilliant," said God. "That's what I'll do. I will become bread so that when humans eat it they will know that I am always with them and that I love them."

And so he did!

Bread Blessed and Broken
(John 6:1-15, 22-71)

Matthew, Mark and Luke tell us that Jesus changed bread and wine into his Body and Blood. At the Last Supper he told his disciples what they were to do in memory of him: They were to take bread and table wine, bless them and repeat his words "This is my body. This is my blood" (see Mark 14:22-25, Matthew 26:26-28, Luke 22:19-20). In his long narration of the words of Jesus at the Last Supper, John does not give an account of Jesus instituting the Eucharist. Scholars think that the story of the multiplication of the loaves was meant to be sufficient explanation of the Eucharist for John's community.

In fact, this miracle is recorded six times in the Gospels. Matthew and Mark each offer two incidents of a large crowd being miraculously fed. Scholars think that all six stories, although they differ in minor details, refer to the same event but that Matthew and Mark offer two slightly different versions: one that developed among Jewish Christians and the other among Gentile Christians. They each put both of them in their Gospels because they saw value and meaning in both versions.

In any case, this story is especially important because it is the only miracle recorded in all four Gospels. Evidently it was burned deeply into the consciousness of the early Christian community because of its close relationship to Jesus' actions at the Last Supper and its echoes of Exodus.

The Book of Exodus is a gripping story of the liberation of a people. The story of their flight through the waters of the Red Sea, starving in the desert, being miraculously fed by the manna they found each morning on the desert floor, receiving the commandments through Moses on a mountain and finally crossing the Jordan into the promised land was etched into the memories of succeeding generations.

Jesus and John were brought up on these stories. They were devout Jews whose ways of thinking, of seeing and interpreting life were conditioned by these stories. It is no wonder that we find echoes of the Exodus at a turning point in Jesus' ministry.

Like Moses he gives the people a miraculous food. Like Moses he teaches them. Moses laid a challenge before his people, "I have set before you life and death, blessings and curses. Choose life so that your descendants may live..." (Deuteronomy 30:19b). And Jesus asks the apostles, "Do you also wish to go away?" (6:67).

The pivotal section on the Bread of Life (John 6) covers two days in the life of Jesus. He feeds the crowd on one afternoon, walks on the water during the night and explains the meaning of the miracle the next day. To understand this story it is important to recognize that this incident is another sign that calls the disciples to faith.

John depicts Jesus in control of a very difficult situation. Looking at the large crowd who were hungry at the end of the day, Jesus puts a perfectly normal question to Philip, "Where are we to buy bread for these people to eat?" (6:5). John immediately says that Jesus knew the answer to the question before he asked it: "He said this to test him, for he himself knew what he was going to do" (6:6).

The disciples' answers to his question were normal. Philip said that they did not have enough money to buy the necessary amount of bread. Andrew said that the supplies on hand, five loaves and two fish, were not sufficient for so many. But when Jesus told the disciples to have the people prepare for supper by sitting down, they did it even though they had no idea where the food was to come from. They obeyed because they trusted Jesus.

In this simple act of obeying Jesus and telling the people to sit down, the disciples demonstrated the Christian faith response to Jesus' commands. First they did what he told them to do in spite of the fact that it seemed foolish and unreasonable to ask people to prepare to eat when there was no food. Then they left the rest to Jesus.

Jesus did not disappoint them. He "took the loaves, and when he had given thanks, he distributed them..." (6:11a). These words are the focal point of the story because they prefigured what the other evangelists tell us Jesus did at the Last Supper (and what the Christian community has been doing ever since): taking bread, blessing it and distributing it.

The story continues on the next day. The crowd has hunted down Jesus on the other side of the lake, looking for another free meal. Perhaps they were hoping that, like Moses in the desert, he would give them a miraculous food that they could gather each day without working for it.

But Jesus disappointed them. They asked for another sign and he merely explained the sign he had already given them. Jesus took the physical bread they had eaten the day before and said it was symbol of a deeper reality: that he, the bread come from heaven, would do for those who believed what ordinary bread did for people's physical bodies.

His listeners knew that bread is the staff of life, that it nourishes life and that without it one dies. By claiming that he is the bread that comes down from heaven, Jesus was saying that it is he who nourishes the new life that will be fulfilled in eternal life. But they have to believe and accept him. The people ask, quite logically, "How can this man give us his flesh to eat?" (6:52b). At this point Jesus asserts the necessity of eating his flesh and drinking his blood if one is to have life that will last forever.

Few Believed

Although before this day there had been some strong opposition to Jesus from a certain group of people, great numbers of ordinary people looked to him as a great teacher, perhaps a prophet or even the Messiah. They were ready to follow him gladly if he gave them an unmistakable sign that he was from God. On the day he fed them with only five loaves of bread and two fish the people said, "This is indeed the prophet who is to come into the world" (6:14b).

But the implications of miraculous multiplication did not sink in. In symbolic language that was difficult to comprehend Jesus assured the people that the God who had protected and nourished them in the past was doing the same now, but in a much more wonderful manner. In the days of old God had spoken only to Moses, but now God was speaking directly to them. In the days of old God's presence was known to the people in a cloud by day and a pillar of fire by night. Now God's presence would be felt and known day by day in the bread of life.

Just as the Israelites had to believe that God was with them in their desperate flight to freedom, so too those who seek the freedom of new life have to believe Jesus is with them in their efforts to become free. Jesus was assuring those who accepted him that he would continue to be among them, continue to nourish them, continue to bring them to freedom and safety. Unlike Moses, whose work for the people ceased at his death, Jesus would be with them as living bread.

Jesus was calling the gathered crowd to see beyond the material reality of bread to something deeper and more real—the presence of the ever-faithful God—and to choose between belief and unbelief, between acceptance and rejection. Most could not see beyond what their senses could perceive. They could not believe and accept Jesus so they rejected him. Only a few could stay and listen further.

At the end of this episode we can picture Jesus seated with the Twelve, watching people shaking their heads in disbelief and slowly wandering down the road to their homes. We can see him looking at the Twelve. He makes no effort to clarify or explain what he said, but he asks, "Do you also want to leave?" He has said what he had to say and they are free to pack up and go home.

Peter gives the perfect response: "Lord, to whom can we go? You have the words of eternal life. We have come to believe and know that you are the Holy One of God" (6:68b-69). Peter's response shows that there is no need to run from one guru to another, from one program to another, from one group to another, looking for easy fixes to life's problem or for something that will give meaning to an often boring existence. For Peter and for the other faithful disciples, as for all people of faith, the meaning of life is found in Jesus Christ, the one who has come from God.

Today this passage poses a similar challenge to the reader. Obviously Jesus did not intend a cannibalistic meal. But in light of the Last Supper, he did mean that when we eat the bread and drink the wine he is in some mysterious and wonderful way truly present and united with us.

There are three basic responses to it: (1) to see it as a hard saying and dismiss Jesus because he seems to be talking nonsense; (2) to say that we believe but that the bread and wine are only a symbol of Jesus; (3) to take his words literally and to believe that Jesus is indeed present in the Eucharist under the appearances of bread and wine.

If we profess the third answer to the question, we may have to ask how we show that belief in practice, because what we do day by day may give the lie to our words. Belief in the real presence of Jesus shows itself in the way we pray before and after receiving Communion. It manifests itself by the reverence we show to the Blessed Sacrament entering and leaving Church. Perhaps the practice that best shows the depth of our belief in the eucharistic presence of Christ is the effort we make to go to Mass. Do we go regularly out of habit, out of fear or out of faith in the presence and action of Jesus?

If we do not go regularly, why not? People who do not attend Mass on a weekly or daily basis usually have an excuse. They are too busy. They find that the homily or the way the Mass is celebrated does nothing for them. No matter the excuse, the basic reason is a weak faith or a lack of faith either in Jesus or in his real presence.

In the history of the Church there are stories of people doing heroic things in order to have the Eucharist. For example, several centuries ago in England and Ireland, and just seventy years ago when there was a persecution in Mexico and priests were being hunted by the police, people would risk imprisonment and death by hiding priests in their homes so that they could have the Mass now and then.

This deep faith is also shown by the extraordinary efforts people everywhere make to attend Mass and receive the Lord. A woman whose husband left her with three children under ten had to take two jobs to make ends meet. Yet for years no matter how late she got to bed she rose for the six-thirty Mass. Now that the boys are grown and she is retired, she says that she could not have done it without the strength she received from the Eucharist each day.

The faith was shown in a slightly different way by a woman who had a small daughter terminally ill with cancer. The mother sought all the medical help she could find—surgery, radiation, chemotherapy—all to no avail. As the child grew weaker and weaker, the priest who visited her noticed one day that there was a decided turn for the worst and that death was near. The mother mentioned that the child had not made her First Communion. The priest offered to say Mass in the home the following day and to give the child her First Communion.

During the silence before the Closing Prayer the priest overheard the mother quietly praying, "Thank you, Lord, for allowing my daughter to have your greatest gift." After Mass she told the priest that she knew that there was no more that she could do for her daughter now that the child had met Jesus in the Eucharist. The child died in two days, and the mother was at peace.

FOR REFLECTION

1) *The Gospel of John contains many allusions to the events and words of the Old Testament. Some Bibles indicate these in footnotes. Do you ever look up these references? If so, in what way do they enrich your understanding of the New Testament texts?*

2) *What do you believe about the Eucharist? Is it merely a memorial service of Jesus? A symbol of him? His real presence? If the last, how do you show your belief in that presence?*

3) *What does this account of the multiplication of the loaves and Jesus' sermon afterward suggest to you about the nature of God?*

4) *In what way do you see the Eucharist as the bread of life for you?*

Walking on Water (John 6:16-21)

Between the multiplication of the loaves and the sermon on the bread of life, John relates another episode that called for faith and trust from the disciples. After the crowd had been fed Jesus went off to pray. The disciples got into their boat and set out across the lake. A squall came up. The boat was in danger of swamping because of the strong wind. These men knew the sea. A high wave could easily engulf their boat, which was no more than a large rowboat.

Then they saw someone walking on the water. They were fishermen. They knew that people swim or sink in the sea, but that they do not walk upon it. They became afraid because they thought they were seeing a ghost or some preternatural vision, but it was Jesus. He read their fear and assured them by saying "It is I."

This is the fifth sign that John records. It shows Jesus' power over nature. He was doing something totally opposite to all physical laws. His statement of identity showed that he was exercising the power of God. Literally his words "It is I" can be translated "I AM," which was the name God gave when Moses asked in whose presence he stood (see Exodus 3:13-15). Jesus was assuring the men in the boat that the God of power and might was with them when they were in darkness and afraid because of the turmoil around them. He was calling them to trust him even when things were darkest.

FOR REFLECTION

1) *When did some unexpected person come to your rescue when your life was in turmoil?*

2) *What does this episode suggest to you about the way God treats us during times of trial and suffering?*

Chapter Six

The Growing
Opposition to Jesus

"THE MORE THINGS CHANGE, the more they remain the same." A good example of this old saying can be found by comparing our celebration of Memorial Day with the ancient Jewish Feast of Tabernacles. Both were established for a purpose and both acquired different meanings over time.

Decoration Day was established in 1868 to honor those who died in the Civil War. In succeeding years other Americans died in other wars. The name of the holiday was changed to Memorial Day and now the day honors those who died in all our country's wars rather than merely the dead of the Civil War. But in the popular mind Memorial Day has acquired still another meaning: It signals the end of the school year and the beginning of the summer vacation. Who knows what other events Americans in the year 2195 will be celebrating on the last Monday in May?

Something similar happened over the centuries with the Feast of Tabernacles. Scholars think that this feast was originally a Middle Eastern agricultural festival celebrated at the end of September and the beginning of October. It was a time to sing, dance, feast and thank the gods for the grain and the grapes that were being gathered. It was also a time to ask for the rain necessary for good crops in the coming year.

The Israelites took over this festival from their pagan neighbors and over the centuries added other meanings to it. Early in Scripture it was a time to renew the covenant Yahweh had made with the people at Sinai. Centuries later it also came to commemorate the dedication of Solomon's temple. At some unknown date the feast also became a memorial of the time the Israelites wandered for forty years in the desert, living in tents. Thus it was likewise known as the Feast of Booths (Huts), because it was customary for people to build huts of branches in which they were to live during the week-long celebration. This custom may have developed from the practice of building such small huts and living in the fields during harvesttime to protect their crops. Later generations added a religious meaning to this practice.

The Clash in the Temple (John 7:1-52)

The Feast of Tabernacles was half over when Jesus went up to the temple and began to teach. Some people were enthralled by his words, but his enemies' reaction was to question his credentials. They wanted to know where and how he had been educated because he did not follow the customary teaching method of the rabbis, which was to quote other rabbis, those who had taught them and those from long ago. He spoke on his own.

The dialogue got a bit heated. Jesus told them that his teaching came from above but then he charged them with trying to kill him. Instead of trying to understand and digest his reply they immediately denied the accusation: "You have a demon! Who is trying to kill you?" (7:20).

In this exchange we can see many of the religious controversies that began in the past and go on in our day— charges, countercharges and accusations while the point under discussion is ignored. When people began to think that perhaps Jesus might be right and began to believe in him, his opponents turned to force and tried to arrest him.

The reason they failed, according to John, was that Jesus' time had not yet come. He was in control of the situation.

It is difficult to identify the motives of those individuals whom John calls "the Jews." They certainly were not all the people. From other incidents we know that some of Jesus' opponents were concerned about their position, their power and their relationship with the Romans.

Because human nature does not change all that much, we can speculate that others were rigid types who could see things only one way and who strongly resisted anyone or anything that smacked of change. They were set in their understanding of what God is like. They were not open to a wider and deeper concept of God's nature. They thought that their understanding of the Scriptures was absolute and unchangeable.

The conflict between new ideas and established systems is among the oldest human dilemma. People in the Church today face this dilemma. They think that what they learned as children was cast in concrete and that no one can change it. The dogmas of the Church are unchangeable, but they can also be developed and more deeply understood. Many other things in the Church are only custom and can change. Yet for some people the established system is sacrosanct. They cannot tolerate anyone who expresses ideas in a different way or who wants to change practices even for good and solid reasons.

A priest recently told of meeting a woman of this mindset. On Easter Sunday he had hung a large tapestry of the risen Christ on the back wall of the sanctuary, covering the dead body of Christ on the crucifix. He wanted to show visually and vividly that Easter celebrated Christ's resurrection from the dead. His homily centered on this idea.

After Mass an irate woman approached him and demanded that the crucifix be uncovered to show the dead Christ. The pastor patiently explained why the crucifix was covered and that the crucifix would be unveiled again when Ordinary Time resumed after Pentecost. His reasoned explanation seemed only to deepen the lady's resolve. With fire in her eyes she blurted out, "I don't care about Ordinary Time! I want him back now, dead on the cross!"

One of the ceremonies conducted during the Feast of Tabernacles was a pouring out of water, a symbol of God giving life. This ceremony had its origin in an ancient rite asking God for rain during the coming year. On each of the seven days of the feast the priests and people would go in procession to the fountain of Gihon, from which came the waters for the pool of Siloam. The priests would fill a golden pitcher with water, carry it to the temple and pour it over the southwest corner of the Altar of Holocausts (the direction from which the rains came) onto the ground.

Jesus took advantage of the situation to foretell his death and to call the people to come to him and drink of the waters of life.

> On the last day of the festival, the great day, while Jesus was standing there, he cried out, "Let anyone who is thirsty come to me, and let the one who believes in me drink. As the Scripture has said, 'Out of the believer's heart shall flow rivers of living water.' " (7:37-38)

John then explains that Jesus was referring to the Holy Spirit, who would flow from Jesus to those who believe in him (7:39).

The symbolism of living water (water that flows and is fresh, not stagnant or brackish) brings to mind the life-giving power of God, who gave water from a rock to save his people from dying of thirst in the desert (Exodus 17:1-6). It evokes images of the day of God's final victory as pictured by the prophets Joel (3:18) and Ezekiel (47:1-12), when rivers of water flowing from the city and from the temple give life to all the land and people. The prophets pictured the Day of the Lord as the day when God would overcome all the foes of Israel and make it a great and glorious kingdom.

The Day of the Lord has come in the death and resurrection of Jesus, not in a military victory. Living water, the Holy Spirit, has flowed from his side on the cross to bring life to all those who will receive it. The image of the trees that Ezekiel pictures growing along the banks of this new and mighty river suggest the impact of the Holy Spirit on a person's life:

> On the banks on both sides of the river, there will grow all kinds of trees for food. Their leaves will not wither nor their fruit fail, but they will bear fresh fruit every month, because the water for them flows from the sanctuary. Their fruit will be for food, and their leaves for healing (47:12).

The life that the Spirit pours into a person will be everlasting. It will be a life that exists not for itself—its own peace, its own happiness, its own health—but a life that will continually feed, nourish and cure those who come in contact with it, who eat of its fruit. The beauty and goodness of this symbolic river conveys better than words the idea of a good, generous, benevolent God.

In this day and age it is difficult to appreciate that faith in Jesus, who is sent from the Father and who shares his Spirit, is the way to obtain the peace and good life conveyed by the metaphor of living water. Advertising and the media incessantly tell us that abundant life, full life, the good life comes from things, not from the Spirit. The more we have, the more we buy, the more life we will have. Personal growth programs hold forth the promise that if we do certain exercises or think certain thoughts, our lives will be full and rewarding. Yet Jesus pinpoints the one thing essential for a full and rewarding life: faith in him that opens our hearts to the Holy Spirit.

FOR REFLECTION

*1) Most believers will experience at some time in their
lives some resistance to the teachings of Jesus. What do*

you think is most often the cause of that resistance: ignorance or lack of understanding of what he taught, rigid ideas that his words challenge, self-interest of some sort, some other reason?

2) *In your own life how have you experienced Jesus as a river of flowing water?*

3) *What does this confrontation between Jesus and his opponents suggest to you about the way God deals with those who are opposed to him?*

'Stone Her!' (John 8:1-11)

John says that Jesus left the temple and went to the Mount of Olives. Perhaps he went to pray. In any case, his enemies were at it again the next day. They thought they had him on the horns of a dilemma. They asked him what should be done about a woman caught in adultery. If he said to stone her as the law demanded, he would get in trouble with the Romans, who allowed the Jews to live by their own laws but reserved capital punishment to themselves. If he said to let her go, they could say he had no respect for the law of Moses. Jesus chose neither answer. He merely said, "Let anyone among you who is without sin be the first to throw a stone at her" (8:7b).

This story poses a real problem for people who look upon the printed word in their Bible as the ultimate and independent norm of revelation. It is a problem for some Scripture scholars as well. The problem for the first group comes from the fact that some modern translations of the Bible omit the story entirely because it is not found in the earliest texts. Other Bibles put it in brackets, indicating that it is not part of the original book because in some ancient manuscripts the story is found at the end of the Gospel of John and in others it is found in Luke. The problem for these people is which Bible is the authentic word of God, the one

72

with the story or the one without it? For Catholics, this is not a problem because the Church has accepted it in its present position as the word of God.

There is, however, a problem for scholars, who have to try to explain why some copyists omitted it and others included it, and why still others placed it in different spots in their manuscripts. Some scholars think the story was omitted because of the controversy that raged in the Church during the first two or three centuries as to whether serious sins such as murder, adultery and idolatry could be forgiven if committed after Baptism. Some people said, "No! Never!" Others said, "Only on one's death bed." Still others said, "Yes—but once, not twice." Some copyists may have dropped this story from the manuscript because it seemed to depict the Lord as too lenient toward sinners.

The simplest and most obvious explanation as to why the story was not part of many early manuscripts is that it is an authentic account of Jesus' words and actions that was preserved by tradition in another source, another set of notes than what John used. In time the copyists realized that this was an authentic story about Jesus and incorporated it into John's Gospel. The Church has accepted it as part of that Gospel.

In any case, the story as it is now placed in the Gospel fits very well because it is another instance of the growing opposition to Jesus that John has been depicting for several chapters. This opposition was growing in intensity. In John 5 we read how the persecution of Jesus began because he cured a man on the sabbath. In John 6 we read that some of Jesus' disciples left him because he called himself the bread of life who came down from heaven and who gives eternal life. In John 7, the Pharisees send police to the temple to arrest Jesus as he preaches, but they hesitate because "Never has anyone spoken like this!" Nicodemus tried to get a fair hearing for Jesus but he was dismissed with a sarcastic remark: "Surely you are not also from Galilee, are you? Search and you will see that no prophet is to arise from Galilee" (7:52).

Now the opposition is growing. In this story the actual plotting against Jesus begins. It will end when his enemies bribe Judas to betray him so that they can have him put to death.

These stories of the growing opposition to Jesus are not a mere recital of historical facts. They are symbolic of the fact that not all people accepted him. They show that some people had and still have a violent opposition to Jesus, that their hearts are closed to him, that they refuse the light and life that he offers.

The men who dragged the woman for judgment by Jesus show an attitude that helps explain why people then and now refuse to accept his offer. They were not really concerned that the woman had sinned, that she had broken the law. Nor did they understand the prophets, who called all sin adultery because by it people were being unfaithful to God. They knew the letter of the law and they were using it not to bring the woman to repentance, but to further their own ends: namely, to trap a man who was threatening their way of thinking and their way of life.

When Jesus pointed out that they should look at themselves in a different way, that they should see themselves as sinners like the woman, they were in effect being given a choice. They could be open to a new and different way of looking at the failings of others and to a new way of seeing their need for God, or they could remain in their self-centered and righteous opposition to Jesus. They closed their minds and hearts and chose to go home and plot how to remove this thorn from their midst. This trick of using the word of God for one's own ends and of being absolutely positive of one's own way of understanding and interpreting that word may still be found today in those who profess belief in Jesus. Today as then it militates against the growth and flowering of the new life offered by Jesus.

When we look beneath the surface of this confrontation, we find the face of a God too good to be true. A sinner who seems to deserve severe punishment is let off without judgment and with only a warning not to sin again.

Jesus still shows that face to sinners in the Sacrament of Reconciliation. Mike had been away from the Church for forty-five years. Someone brought him to a parish group that discussed the Scriptures for the upcoming Sunday. After a time he made up his mind to be reconciled with God and the Church. When his friends playfully asked what he was so worried about, he rolled his eyes and replied, "What haven't I done?" Finally, just before Christmas, he entered the confessional with fear and trepidation. When he finished his story he waited for the expected scolding. But all the priest did was put his hand on his shoulder and say, "Buddy, you've made my day."

Scripture says that God is just. We humans expect that justice to be an exact reckoning for every large and small infraction of the law. God is just in that God always acts out of the divine nature: out of love, never out of a spirit of vengeance. Because the new life Jesus shares with us liberates the heart from the hardness that makes it impervious to the Father's merciful love, it must be a life of forgiveness. Forgiveness is liberating not only to the one who is forgiven but also—even more so—to the one who forgives. The life Jesus calls people to is a life of freedom and broad vision. Refusing to forgive, clinging to the injury, restricts one's freedom and narrows one's vision. Non-forgiveness means clinging to the mistakes of the past.

In a lecture on the spiritual interpretation of Scripture, Father John Shea once explained the binding effect of not forgiving and the freeing effect of forgiving. It goes something like this: When I look at you I see you through the mental image I have in my mind. If I do not forgive you, your mistake, your fault, your sin becomes the focal point of my image of you, the lens that colors and distorts what I see. I keep it in the forefront of my consciousness. I remember it each time I look at you. I freeze you in that instant of your life. That memory distorts all that you say and do from then on. I find it almost impossible to see you in a different light, to understand you better, to draw closer to you.

When I am in this situation two choices face me. On one hand, I can keep you locked in that instant. In so doing I am binding myself to one way of seeing and relating to you and my freedom is lessened. When I hold you in your fault I am binding myself to my fault. In effect, this means that when others see my faults, they should hold me bound by them as I am holding you bound to your fault. The two of us are now in the same boat: being judged and rejected. The accusers held the woman taken in adultery bound and subject to judgment. In so doing they bound themselves and made themselves subject to judgment.

On the other hand, I can let go of that image and free you. In so doing I also free myself to look at my own faults and mistakes and to realize that I too am weak and flawed. I free myself to new ways of looking at the hurtful situations I have caused.

Forgiveness does not mean that I wipe the incident out of my mind. It happened and I did feel the hurt. But I see it in a different way, especially as a way to imitate a loving and forgiving Father. I see that my life is showing the fruits of being joined with Jesus, because when I forgive I am most like him.

Once I learn how to forgive in one case I become more free to forgive "seventy-seven times" (see Matthew 18:21-22). I am free to see the goodness lurking in the other just as Jesus saw it in the woman when he said, "Neither do I condemn you. Go your way, and from now on do not sin again" (John 8:11b).

One might argue that these words were easy for Jesus to say because sin was not a direct wound to him. Words are cheap in cases like that. This objection is answered in the words Jesus spoke on the cross when the very persons who inflicted pain and certain death on him came to taunt and revile him. That occasion was the test for him. What would he do? Return violence for violence or forgive as he had done and had asked Peter to do? The answer is in Luke's account of the crucifixion: "Father, forgive them; for they do not know what they are doing" (Luke 23:34).

Forgiveness also offers freedom to the one who is forgiven. If someone points out how I have failed, what hurt I have inflicted, and then forgives me, I am free to look at what I said or did without trying to justify or defend myself. I may see myself in a different light and make the effort to change. I may also learn how to forgive those who have hurt me. Often I may feel a bond with the person who forgives because I know that he or she has seen the dark side of my character and still cares for me. This type of caring and loving is most liberating.

At one level the story of the woman taken in adultery is about the people who opposed Jesus and who were trying to trip him up. At another level it is about God's compassion for sinners, shown through the words and actions of Jesus. At still another level it is symbolic of the way forgiveness works to free ourselves and others to live the life Christ offers us.

FOR REFLECTION

1) *Why does the fact that this story is not in all the early manuscripts pose a problem for people who say that the Bible as we have it is the only norm for our faith?*

2) *What are the advantages and disadvantages of the attitude toward sinners found in the way Jesus treated the woman and the way some people in the early Church wanted adulterers treated?*

3) *How do people today use religion for their own particular ends?*

4) *What makes forgiveness so difficult?*

5) *Share and discuss an incident when forgiving another or being forgiven by another has had a freeing and*

life-giving effect on you.

The Light of the World (8:12-51)

After dealing with the opponents who had dragged the woman caught in adultery to him, Jesus again went to the temple to enlighten people about who he was. Each evening during the Feast of Tabernacles four huge golden candlesticks were lit in the Court of the Women to illumine the temple area. Jesus proclaimed that his light did not illuminate a physical area but all of life: "I am the light of the world. Whoever follows me will never walk in darkness but will have the light of life" (8:12b).

Light is a sign of hope and of life. A light in a window guides the lost traveler. Sometimes that light is very small and easily dismissed, but it still holds out hope—as seen in the story of an American airman shot down in Vietnam early in the war.

In the course of his imprisonment he spent six months in solitary confinement in a tiny cell without any light. For the first few weeks he thought he would go crazy. He began to hear voices and was overwhelmed by anxiety attacks. Lying on the floor one day, he pressed his face in desperation against the corner of the cell. He thought he saw a speck of light from the outside through one eye. A minute crack in the wall allowed a splinter of light to enter his cell.

He moved as close as he could to the crack and focused all his energy and attention on that sliver of light. As he strained to see out through that tiny chink, the only thing he could make out was one tiny blade of grass. The sunlight made that single blade of grass sparkle. Each day he would go to that tiny peephole and watch the miracle of that single blade of grass. In the presence of that tiny sign of life he began to think about how God had blessed him in many ways, especially through those who loved him.

Slowly his mind began to clear. His thoughts turned to

the power of God at work in that tiny blade of grass. He could feel his energy and his hope slowly returning and growing each day. His anxiety faded and he found peace of mind and heart.

After his release from the P.O.W. camp three years later, he remarked that one crack of light and one tiny blade of grass saw him though the terrible darkness of solitary confinement.

It is this power of light that Jesus captured when he claimed to be the light of the world. Light cuts through darkness, revealing what is hidden or not clearly discerned. Jesus is the light that constantly probes and penetrates the darkness of ignorance that keeps God hidden—or at least shrouded. Jesus is the light that helps us understand and appreciate the life God is willing to share with us.

The motif of light and darkness in John expresses two worlds. One offers a clear vision of who we are and of our destiny: the life God shares with us. The other is a life lived in the dark of sin and evil, which blinds us to the reality of God, to Jesus and to our true nature.

Most people make their way through life at times in the light and at other times plunging into the dark, heedless of the consequences of such a choice. Jesus could readily say that he judges no one because he lays before each person a choice between light and darkness. A person is already judged by the choices he or she makes. Some lead to the light and to God's life. Others lead to darkness and the absence of that life now and for eternity.

The people around Jesus—even those who were his disciples—did not understand what he was trying to convey to them. They asked him once again who he was. He told them how they would recognize him: "When you have lifted up the Son of Man, then you will realize that I am he, and that I do nothing on my own, but I speak these things as the Father instructed me" (8:28). (He was, of course, referring to his death on the cross and his resurrection.) Time after time he tried to convince people of who he was and what his mission was. Finally, when pressed hard by his opponents he repeated his claim to be "I AM," applying to himself the holy name that the Jews used for God.

The root of this name is the verb *to be*. It can be understood in several ways. God's answer to Moses' request for his name was "I am who (what) I am" or "I will be (what) I will be" (see Exodus 3:13-15). In other places the name connotes divine mystery and freedom or divine presence. It could mean, "He causes to be what exists," meaning that God is the Creator and Ruler of history.

Whatever the root of the word, whatever meaning it had in the minds of the people, they realized that Jesus was putting himself on a par with God, taking God's name for his own. He makes this claim to everyone who reads John's Gospel. It is the key to the choice presented to the reader: Believe and find life and freedom. Quibble, argue, doubt, refuse to believe and enter a life of darkness and slavery.

The choice is between freedom and slavery. Accepting Jesus and doing his word frees one from despair, from being overly anxious about life, from seeing nothing but darkness in the future, from lack of purpose, from our own destructive desires. Rejecting Jesus' claim means turning away from the Father, silencing God's voice in one's heart and embracing self-centeredness—sin—which enslaves even when it is sought in the name of freedom.

Many of Jesus' hearers evidently did not accept him. Nor do they seem to have walked away still keeping the question open. No, they closed their minds to him—and they did not stop there. They began to plot to kill him. They succeeded in their plans, but their success was only temporary, because by their action they gave him the opportunity to perform the sign that made him publicly known to all peoples and manifested his power and glory to the world.

While it is true that Jesus' sermons on the occasion of the Feast of Tabernacles are about himself, they are, at a more fundamental level, about who God is. When he says, "I am the light," he is also talking about his Father as the source of all life, the light that dispels the darkness of sin, the God who speaks the truth that frees people from the slavery of sin, the God who sends and authenticates a man so that those who believe can know him and share in his life.

People respond to that God today as they did in the time of Jesus. Many people are content to stumble on in the darkness of ignorance and their own preconceived ideas about God. Others are outright hostile and try to destroy the God Jesus came to reveal. They cannot kill God as his enemies killed Jesus, but they can obscure and even blot out his image by their philosophical reflections. Others cannot accept the God Jesus reveals as real. They seek God in exotic places and esoteric ways. They go to gurus in far-off lands. They delve into mysterious religious practices. They use drugs or items that they believe have magical or mystical qualities.

To all these people Jesus cries in a loud voice something like this: "No! No! Look at me! Learn of me! I am the light of life. You see me. You see the Father from whom I have come. In accepting me, you accept the Father and have truth and life!"

The light that Jesus sheds on God is not the blinding light from which Moses had to shield his eyes when he went up on Mount Sinai to meet God (see Exodus 24:15-18). It is a clear, warm light that reveals a loving Father, a self-sacrificing brother and a gentle guiding Spirit. It is a light into which we can look directly and cry, "*Abba*, Father!" It is a light that reveals the kind of life this loving Father wills to share with us and points out the pitfalls that can snuff out that life.

Those who listened to Jesus in the temple were uncertain about who he was. "While some were saying, 'He is a good man,' others were saying, 'No, he is deceiving the crowd' " (John 7:12b). This uncertainty and the controversies to which it gives rise continue to this day. Although people of many faiths believe that Jesus is a good man, a great

81

teacher, even a prophet, millions of others think he is leading people astray because they believe in one God and do not see how Jesus can be the Son of God, equal to the Father. Because Jesus claims to have seen the Father and to have been sent by him, the controversy goes beyond the person of Jesus and extends to belief in God. Some people see Jesus as a good man showing them that there is a God and the kind of God he is. Others—militant atheists, dedicated Marxists, materialists and indifferent agnostics—see him as a man leading people astray by his assertions that there is a God who is good and caring.

FOR REFLECTION

1) *When during your life have you walked in darkness? How did the light of Jesus come to clarify the path you needed to take?*

2) *In what ways do you see darkness coming into the world?*

3) *In what ways do you see the light of Jesus penetrating that darkness?*

Chapter Seven
A Persistent God

JESUS WAS VERY PERSISTENT. Time and time again he failed to convince the crowd—and especially the Pharisees—of who he was and of what he was about. Over and over he called them to faith and invited them to discipleship and they closed their ears. Nonetheless, he tried again whenever the opportunity presented itself. He did not give up even when it was obvious that people's minds and hearts were closed to his words.

In the first verse of his poem "The Hound of Heaven," Francis Thompson depicts the hardened heart seeking to avoid God, the Hound persistently pursuing his quarry:

> I fled Him, down the nights and down the days;
> I fled Him down the arches of the years;
> I fled Him down the labyrinthine ways
>   Of my own mind; and in the mist of tears
> I hid from Him, and under running laughter.
>   Up vistaed hopes I sped;
>   and shot, precipitated;
>   Adown Titanic glooms of chasmèd fears,
> From those strong Feet that followed, followed after.
>   But with unhurrying chase,
>   and unperturbèd pace,
>   Deliberate speed, majestic instancy,
>   They beat—and a Voice beat
>   More instant than the Feet—
>   "All things betray thee, who betrayest Me."

The Good Shepherd (John 10:1-39)

After Jesus had cured the man born blind and after the tumult caused by that miracle had died down (John 9), Jesus tried once more to enlighten a group of Pharisees who claimed that they were not blind, that they could recognize the truth. Even though they professed to be open to hearing what Jesus had to say, the Gospel reveals that they had from the beginning been creating mental blocks that prevented them from any objective evaluation of his words.

When Jesus chased the merchants and money changers out of the temple (John 2:13-22), those who were not friendly to him demanded a sign that he had the authority to do what he had done. Their attitude was that only those in charge of the temple had a right to say what went on in it.

This attitude was more clearly manifested when they called Jesus a lawbreaker and questioned by what authority he cured on the sabbath (5:1-30). They were blocked in the way they saw people. They looked at everyone who came along through the eyes of the law instead of through the life and words of that person.

A little later their attitude about the importance of formal learning blocked them from hearing and appreciating what Jesus was saying. "How does this man have such learning when he has never been taught?" (7:15b). These Pharisees were steeped in the human attitude of being unable to hear truth from someone different from themselves. Status, money and education prevented them from giving Jesus a fair hearing. They felt that he was a threat to their values and view of life, so they argued with him, dismissed him and rejected him.

When these Pharisees denied that they were blind, Jesus asserted that they were indeed blind, but once again tried to explain his identity. He used a comparison that all his listeners could easily grasp to illustrate his role: He was a shepherd who knew each sheep by name. (Shepherds had a close relationship with their sheep. They usually had only a few to care for and these often were the family's main asset. An individual sheep usually had a name, and its needs and characteristics were well known to the one who looked after the tiny flock.) This shepherd had access to the common fenced-in area where the sheep of several flocks were kept at night.

This comparison may not be as illuminating to us as it would have been to first-century people, because so few of us have had firsthand experience with shepherds and sheep. We may have seen shepherds with their flocks on TV, but we have not tended sheep ourselves or lived in close proximity with those who have done so.

Neither do most of us grasp the way the prophets and the psalms spoke of God's protective love and guidance in terms of shepherd and sheep. As Jesus spoke, perhaps the words of Psalm 23 popped into their minds:

> The LORD is my shepherd, I shall not want.
>   He makes me lie down in green pastures;
> he leads me beside still waters;
>   he restores my soul.
> He leads me in right paths.... (Psalm 23:1-3b)

It would have been difficult for those who were well versed in the prophets to miss the connection between Jesus' words about thieves, robbers and worthless hired help and Ezekiel's denunciation centuries before of the faithless leaders of Israel. Jesus' claim to be the Good Shepherd echoed God's promise through Ezekiel to appoint one shepherd to care for and pasture his people (see Ezekiel 34). They would have instantly realized that by speaking of a "good" shepherd he was by implication speaking of "bad" shepherds. This reference should have caused the Pharisees and the religious leaders to evaluate their exercise of leadership, their care of God's flock.

In a way, Jesus was reaching out to them one more time, suggesting that they see themselves in a different light and come to faith in him. But neither Jesus' words nor his inferences enlightened all of his hearers. Instead, they caused more tumult and confusion. Some of those who stood before him said he must be crazy. Others said he could not be because of his healing of the blind man.

Even though the comparison Jesus was making may not have the same impact on us as it would have had on a people raised on the words of the prophets and closely associated with tending sheep, we still can grasp the point he was making: He knows and cares for the individual as well as for the entire flock. He is the Good Shepherd, not a thief or a lazy hired hand.

It is not clear how a shepherd saves his sheep by laying down his life. It seems that he needs to be alert and vigilant in order to fend off marauding bears and wolves. Jesus evidently foresaw that feeding, protecting and guiding his flock would involve his death. From that death would come reconciliation with the Father, along with power and life for those who believe.

Theologians have struggled for centuries to explain how Jesus' death reconciles and gives power and life to his sheep. *That* it does is true. *How* is not that clear. Perhaps another story, this time one from the East, will help us appreciate what Jesus has done for us.

Once there was a marvelous kingdom in a far-off land. It was a rich and fantastic place with a good and kindly king. This king had built himself a special garden unlike any that ever existed. In the garden he planted the most beautiful of all God's flowers and plants. One tree, a tall stately palm that towered above every other tree in the garden, was unique in its beauty. Its fruit was the sweetest anyone had tasted. Its graceful branches whispered a soothing song as they swayed in the breeze. Everyone agreed that there was no other palm tree like this one.

One day as the king walked through his garden he paused at the foot of the palm tree, looked up, and said, "Palm tree, I love you." The palm tree already knew this. He just bowed down gracefully and absorbed the message. The king said as the tree was straightening up, "And I would ask something of you." The tree, who loved the king, said, "Anything you wish." The king said, "I would cut you down!" There was total silence in the garden. Nothing moved! Out of that stillness, ever so faintly came the reply, "If you must, then cut me down."

No sooner had the reply come when the king continued, "Not only must I cut you down, but I must cut you in two." Then even the birds ceased their flying. Out of the silence, again hesitantly and ever so faintly, came the reply, "If you must, then cut me in two." The king, with sorrow and with love in his voice continued, "And I must hollow you out." The tree had no more energy. It simply bowed in submission.

The next day the king's servants came into the garden. They cut down the tree, split it in two and hollowed it out. Then they carried both parts into the field, which that year had become parched for lack of rain. They laid the two sections of the hollowed-out tree end on end from a spring to the dying field. Water flowed from the spring through the hollowed-out tree to the field, and the crop flourished. When harvesttime came, the king and the people of the kingdom enjoyed an abundant crop.

The death/resurrection of the Good Shepherd is more than an example. It is more than a symbol of the many deaths and resurrections we experience during our lives. It is more than a heroic gesture. It did something for the sheep that they could do not do for themselves. It made it possible for the believer to be one with Christ and share in the very life of God. It provided a power for living that is beyond any human power because it makes it possible for us to live as sons and daughters of a caring, provident God. This life cannot be earned. It is not a reward for doing good but a free gift offered to those who accept Jesus. Salvation or redemption means that we have accepted the gift and, with God's help and guidance, live a life that reveals God to others.

John ends this confrontation by saying that Jesus asked these Pharisees once again to accept his works if they could not accept his words. Their response was once again to try to kill him.

But then John shows that fascination with Jesus had led some people to discipleship. Jesus left Jerusalem and went back to the area where John had been baptizing. There he found some who accepted him on the word of John the Baptizer. What they had heard of Jesus' signs and preaching confirmed John's words about him and led them to faith.

Perhaps John the Baptizer led more people to discipleship than Andrew and John. Years later, Paul found in Ephesus disciples who had been baptized only with John's baptism. Saying that John worked no miracles (10:41) indicates that Jesus was greater than the Baptizer because he did work signs. The evangelist takes great pains to show that Jesus was superior to the Baptizer. Some scholars say that for many years after the Resurrection, as many as a hundred or more, there were followers of John the Baptizer who did not accept Jesus. This passage hints at a possible conflict between John's community and followers of the Baptizer.

It is interesting to note that John places many of Jesus' clearest announcements of his identity at the temple on different feasts of the year. At the Feast of Tabernacles Jesus asserted that his message was not his own but that of the one who sent him (John 7). At the Feast of the Dedication (Hanukkah), which celebrates the rededication of the temple after the pagans had been driven from Jerusalem, Jesus speaks of his unity with the Father and of giving eternal life (John 10). Finally, John places Jesus' arrest at the eve of Passover (John 18). Then Jesus told the high priest that he had spoken clearly enough about who he claimed to be; he told Pilate that he was truly a king.

To the Jews the temple was the sign of God's dwelling among them, of divine presence and care. It was only right that Jesus should so strenuously proclaim his identity in that holy place because he was taking over as the sign of God's presence among humans. No longer were people to look to a building to sense the presence of God among them: God is present in the person of Jesus. No beautiful building, no inspiring ritual can replace the person of Jesus as the contact point between humanity and God.

FOR REFLECTION

1) *In your own life or in the lives of people around you, you may have seen some of the attitudes that kept many of the people from believing in and following Jesus. How did these attitudes manifest themselves?*

2) *Describe the image that comes to your mind as you picture a shepherd with his flock. What characteristics would you attribute to the shepherd?*

3) *Recall and share an incident in which someone either physically or metaphorically gave his or her life that another might live.*

4) *For the Jews, the temple was the sign of God's presence among them. Of what is your parish church or St. Peter's in Rome a sign for you?*

'Whoever Believes in Me Believes Not in Me But in Him Who Sent Me.' (John 12:1-44b)

The young man sitting in the priest's office seemed sad. He had just completed four years at a Catholic university and was contemplating what he was going to do with his life. "I came to this Catholic university for an education and to find God," he mused. "I have the education, but I have not found God. I guess I'll have to look someplace else."

The priest said nothing, but wished him Godspeed. The young man flew off to India and there became a disciple of a famous guru. After many months he felt that he was still no closer to finding God than he had been at the university. He took off for a monastery in Tibet and spent many peaceful months there—but he did not find God. He came back to the States, spent some time with Native Americans, looking for the God hidden in nature, but he had no luck.

Finally, he set aside his search and took a job. Some time later he bumped into his priest friend and told him about his search. He had learned a great deal about himself, the young man admitted, but God seemed farther way, less clear and more vague now than when he had been at the university.

The priest listened and then asked, "Have you ever thought of sitting still and letting God find you?"

The point of this story is obvious. The search for God, for spirituality, for genuine religion depends very little on one's efforts and very much on God's initiative. But the story leaves us up in the air. We do not know whether the young man took the priest's advice or how God found him. Neither do we know how he responded to God's self-revelation.

The story of that disillusioned student is the story of Israel. It is the story of an unimportant small tribe of people and their efforts to find God. Episode after episode in their history shows that when the people sought God on their own, they ended up worshiping the idols of the people among whom they lived. But it also tells the story of how God time and time again contacted them, spoke to them, saved them.

This story is brought to a wonderful climax in the life of Jesus. God's Word, God's revelation, was no longer mediated through the words of prophets and events. God's Word took flesh and lived among the people. In the person of Jesus of Nazareth they could see God.

At the end of the first section of his Gospel the evangelist brings together his themes. The fact that Jesus was always in control of his life and destiny is shown by his response to Judas, who criticized Mary for anointing his feet with expensive perfume (12:1-8). Jesus calls it a preparation for his death, the seed from which much fruit will come.

His mission has not been in vain in spite of all the opposition he has encountered. Many people have been convinced and have believed in him. Even the Gentiles, represented by the Greeks who approached Philip for an audience with Jesus (see 12:20-22), are coming to Jesus. In fact, so many people are attracted to him that certain Pharisees and leaders of the people decide that he must be killed.

Jesus' entry into Jerusalem in triumph and glory (12:12-19) shows that he is indeed Messiah and king but not a worldly leader. Jesus tells the price of discipleship (12:24-28) and once again proclaims that he is the light come into the world from above (12:35-36). He asserts that truly to believe in him is to believe in the Father who sent him. Harking back to the baptism at the Jordan at the beginning of Jesus' mission, the evangelist tells how, near the end of his life, that mission is now validated. Jesus prays, "Father, glorify your name." A voice from heaven, which the crowd hears but does not understand, answers, "I have glorified it and will glorify it again" (see 12:28-29.) And one last time Jesus warns that those who do not accept him or his words will be condemned on the last day (12:48).

The story of the young man and the story of Israel is the story of each one of us. God is reaching out to us. God is talking to us. God is showing us signs if we are not blind or deaf.

For example, through the Gospel of John God is trying to excite our curiosity about Jesus, to help us become so fascinated with him that we are willing to throw our lot in with him and be his disciples. The outcome of this discipleship should be a close, life-giving friendship based on love. Our call ultimately is a call to friendship with God in and through Jesus.

On the surface, the Gospel of John is about Jesus from Nazareth, child of a woman, Messiah, King of Israel, Son of

Man, Son of God. Deeper down this story is about the faithfulness of God. It is about the love, the care and the concern God has for people. It is about the power and glory of God manifested in an unexpected and mystifying way.

The Gospel illustrates how the people who saw and heard Jesus responded to his revelation of God. Some believed and became children of light. Some rejected him outright because their view of what is important blocked them from hearing what Jesus actually was saying. Some said that they believed but straddled the fence and did not have the courage of their convictions. As a result they fell by the wayside when push came to shove. Others were mere bystanders who paid little or no attention to him.

One of the ways we can sit, be quiet and allow God to find us is to hear with an open mind and an open heart the voice of Jesus in the Gospel. This openness requires us to examine our image of God in the light of what we learn from Jesus. If we say that Jesus is like God we are trying to fit Jesus into the image of God we have already formed. Rather we need to say that God is like Jesus. After all, Jesus is the Word become flesh who made his dwelling among us and whose glory we have seen, the glory of the Father's only Son, full of grace and truth (see 1:14).

As a clearer and perhaps different image of God emerges from the Gospel, we should begin to question our previous ideas about who we are, about the purpose of our lives and about the issues of the day (immigration, war, welfare reform, abortion, social justice). Then we can say yes or no—if not in so many words, then at least by our actions— to the Father who sent Jesus to call us.

FOR REFLECTION

This point in the Gospel of John is a good time to pause and ask yourself some of these questions:

1) Jesus was fully human, as we are. He was not a god

*playing at being human. After reading the Gospel thus
far, what do you think are the outstanding personal
characteristics of Jesus?*

*2) Jesus was also fully divine. What do these personal
characteristics say to you about the nature of God?*

*3) In what way has your image of God changed as a result
of reading this Gospel?*

*4) Among the possible ways to respond to Jesus (see pages
79-80), which do you usually take?*

Chapter Eight
Love's Finest Hour

SOME YEARS AGO the official exchange rate for a Soviet ruble was something over $1.15. The unofficial rate in some countries outside the Soviet Union was seventeen cents. One person tells of being told as he was about to leave Russia that he could not take the rubles in his wallet with him when he left. Hurriedly, he gave the pile of ruble notes he had in his pockets to his guide—about two thousand of them. As he rushed to the plane he saw her smiling and heard her call out in amusement, "This is not enough money for a drink."

Language suffers a similar devaluation from indiscriminate use. In time words and phrases used carelessly, out of context and without precision lose or change their meanings. No writing has suffered in this way more than the Scriptures. They were written to inflame the heart and enlighten the mind. Now they often do neither for the skeptic or for the believer.

Perhaps no section of John's Gospel has suffered more in this way than Jesus' sermon at the Last Supper. People glibly flip off remarks about loving one another or giving up one's life for one's friend without understanding or reflecting on what is implied by these words. They forget that knowing the words used to convey religious experience do not necessarily mean possessing the experience behind those words.

Not only do we need to understand religious words,

we need to live them. Understanding the words, while it does not guarantee living by them, is the guide to the kind of life embedded in them. This understanding comes in many ways. In *John*, biblical scholar Gerard Sloyan suggests one way to go about this exploration:

> The inspired prose needs to be dissected or dismantled, each part examined and related to every other, then all polished and reassembled like the parts of a watch if it is to function for the hearer.... No word of the discourse can be treated as an axiom. Unexamined, all the great phrases that have become the world's heritage are like worthless pebbles worn smooth. Without exploration they have no sharp edge, no bite; they challenge the hearer to nothing. Disengaged one from the other, scrutinized under the magnifying glass of faith, they invite the hearer to everything.

The careful dissection and dismantling of these chapters is best left to Scripture scholars and the great spiritual writers. In this case, however, another way to understand the language of Scripture, Jesus' sermon at the Last Supper, is to take an overview of them and concentrate on a few ideas. In this way we may be able to break them open a bit more and get a fresh insight into individual passages and phrases so that they will enlighten our minds and fan the smoldering love in our hearts. Instead of exploring all the ideas contained in Jesus' words at the Last Supper, therefore, we will emphasize just two ideas: the commandments Jesus gave and the aid he promised to help people keep them.

But first, we need a context in which to explore these chapters. In the previous twelve chapters John has shown Jesus calling people to believe in him by telling them time and time again who he is and what he has come to give them: light, life, living water, the bread of life. In these final chapters John masterfully crafts a story that could easily serve as the scenario for a powerful three-act drama entitled *Love's Finest Hour*. In Act One the theme is set: The hero expresses his love for his friends. In Act Two the hero dies. Love seems to have been defeated; the enemy seems to have won. In Act Three that love manifests its power and final victory by overcoming the ultimate enemy, death. The hero rises to eternal glory and shares his victory with the crushed disciples by giving them his own Spirit.

The message of this story burned so deeply in John's heart that for the rest of his life he repeated it over and over again. According to a tradition going back to the third century, when John was an old man living in exile, he repeated this message of love every time he preached. One day when he was being taken to the community's celebration of the Eucharist, some of the young people asked him to preach on a different topic. Kindly, he agreed. When it came time to preach he said, as always, "Little children, love one another." When asked why he had not kept his promise to say something different, he asked, "What else is there to say? The whole message is summed up in that one command of the Lord."

The descendants of these young people still can be found in our churches today. They want the clarity of laws that tell them what they can and cannot do. Homilies on love irritate them. One man was heard to say as he left the church, "Enough of this love stuff! Let's get back to the Commandments!"

Yet "this love stuff" is what John's Gospel is all about. It is more than a command. It is a way of being. It is what it means to be a child of God. It is what it means to be saved. It is what God is. In his last words to his friends, in his last prayer for them and in his death, Jesus was opening his heart to his friends and exposing the love that was there. In so doing, he was also exposing the heart of God and giving them an inkling of what God is really like.

Throughout history gods have been characterized by power and domination. They punish those who oppose them and reward those who appease them. Gods have often enslaved people in superstition and fear. The God whom

Jesus modelled and called Father does not exercise power and domination. This God frees people and allows them to believe or not to believe, to accept or not to accept God, to live by the divine will or not, to love or to ignore God. This God is unconditional love.

It is very comforting to believe in a God of unconditional love who forgives even before forgiveness is asked. But it is deceptive to bask in the love that flows over us without realizing that this love is quite demanding— much more demanding than all the commandments of God and the Church put together. We are to be the conduits of God's love to those around us, just as Jesus was to those around him. It needs to pass through us to others. God's love was spelled out in what Jesus did for us; it calls us to think, judge and act as he did. It is a love that, when accepted, imposes a heavy responsibility because, like Jesus, we are called to mirror the face of a loving God to all we meet each day.

Love Demonstrated and Betrayed (John 13:1-38)

Anyone who has read John thus far might ask, "What must I do to come into the light, to drink of the living water Jesus offered?" The first indication of the answer to that question was given by Mary at the wedding feast at Cana. She told the waiters, "Do whatever he tells you." They did it and a wonderful transformation took place before their eyes.

Mary's instruction to the waiters raises the question, "What did Jesus tell his followers to do in his subsequent years of preaching?" It was more than to fetch some jars of water. The other Gospels have a rather long list of things Jesus told people to do. Matthew, for example, has a long list of do's and don'ts in the Sermon on the Mount (Matthew 5—7). Luke has a similar but shorter list in his Sermon on the

Plain (Luke 6:20-42).

John answers this question in his account of the beautiful, poetic, moving last sermon of Jesus (John 13—21). The rest of his Gospel records very few commands from Jesus. True, in several situations Jesus' words imply a precept. Thus when he says, "Those who eat my flesh and drink my blood abide in me, and I in them" (6:56), he implicitly says that one has to eat his body and drink his blood in order to have the life he has come to share.

Other directives for living in the light can be derived from things Jesus said in particular instances. For example, he told the merchants in the temple, "Stop making my Father's house a marketplace!" (2:16c). He told the woman taken in adultery, "Go your way, and from now on do not sin again" (8:11b). From sayings such as these we can reason that we must have respect for God's house and that we should not sin.

But these directives are not the core of the life Jesus wants his followers to have. Jesus expressed it in three words: "Love one another!" And at the Last Supper he repeated this injunction in three or four different ways.

An eight-year-old boy grasped the meaning of Jesus' words, "No one has greater love than this, to lay down one's life for one's friends" (15:13), even if he was not aware that Jesus had spoken them. His younger sister was dying of a disease from which he had recovered some time before. The doctor told the boy, "Only a transfusion of your blood will save the life of your sister. Are you ready to give her your blood?" The boys' eyes widened in fear. He hesitated a moment or two and then said, "OK, doctor, I'll do it." An hour after the transfusion had been completed the boy hesitantly asked the doctor, "Say, doctor, when do I die?" It was only then that the doctor understood the fear that had seized the boy when he had been asked to give the transfusion. He had thought that in giving his blood he was giving his life for his sister.

The message that Christians have heard from the

beginning—love one another—has not yet penetrated the minds of many of those who profess to be disciples of Jesus. It is truly amazing how many people associate Christian morality with a long list of forbidden fruits and joyless positive obligations. It is natural to want things to be orderly and spelled out so that one can know exactly what is expected, but no law can cover all situations in all cultures for all times. A general principle may seem far too vague to give direction to a particular person in particular situations, but that is what Jesus has left us. He trusts us enough to work out the practical day-to-day applications of his guiding principle.

At the Last Supper, the first way Jesus expressed his fundamental commandment was what he said after he washed the feet of his disciples: "For I have set you an example, that you also should do as I have done to you" (13:15). The washing of feet at the Holy Thursday liturgy, when we hear this charge and see how Jesus demonstrated what he meant, has become so sanitized that it takes a great deal of imagination to realize the kind of service it symbolizes. The priest in his white alb, the server with bowl and towel, the symbolic apostles with clean feet, shined shoes and freshly laundered socks do not accurately portray what Jesus was talking about. Saint Francis embracing the leper, Mother Teresa carrying a filthy dying man to a bed, the Catholic Worker volunteer sitting on the curb talking to a homeless drunk: These people dramatically demonstrate the meaning of Jesus's words.

In a less dramatic way the meaning of these words is illustrated by an incident that occurred at a wedding reception. A couple sat next to a young woman who said that the only person present that she knew was the groom, and that she had just come to town looking for a job and an apartment. They tried to make her feel welcome by talking with her all through the meal. Before the party broke up, the couple put their heads together and decided to invite her to use their spare bedroom until she found an apartment. The young stranger was delighted and stayed with them about two weeks, then went off on her own. Later she wrote to them that she had been turned off on Church, but was having second thoughts because she saw in their home what a Christian family was meant to be. She knew by their concern that they were disciples of Jesus.

Another way of understanding the meaning of Jesus' command is found in a story that has been repeated over and over again since World War II. A small town—some say in Germany, others say in the Philippines—had been heavily bombed. After the American forces took the town, a soldier noticed that the hands had been blown off a statue of Christ with outstretched arms. He printed a crude sign and hung it around the neck of the statue. It read, "Lend me your hands."

Jesus can no longer care for people with dirty, smelly feet in person; we are called to lend him our hands. We are called to care for the sick, especially those who, like the man beside the Bethesda pool, have no one else to help them. We are called to feed the hungry, like those who gathered on the shore of the lake to hear Jesus even when they did not comprehend what he was doing. We are called to forgive, as Jesus forgave the woman taken in adultery.

Jesus' command to love is not restricted to providing for the physical needs of others. It is meant to be a way of life that helps others grow and develop. It is meant to help others become free from fear and learn how to trust the Lord. The opportunities to meet people's physical needs and to free them from injustice and oppression are so numerous that no one can be involved in all of them. But, at the same time, a person who is not involved in at least one such project would do well to meditate each day on Jesus washing the feet of the disciples.

Taking the call for service seriously in one's life often cannot be met in what seems the obvious way. It may require ingenuity and creativity. A religious brother for years visited a state prison and ran a small halfway house for men who had no place to go when released. Finally, burned out, he took a sabbatical. Among other things, he looked into prison ministries around the country. "At first I searched for organizations and structures to help me strategize for prison reform," he says. "I found no Catholic institution concerned enough to put time and money into such a project. Criminal justice is not a serious enough Catholic agenda for the institutional Church. It is an important agenda for the Presbyterians, Quakers and Mennonites."

He was angry and disillusioned. He expected everyone, especially the bishops, to serve by fighting for a Christ-like approach to criminal justice. When he returned home he found that his superior had an idea for a different kind of work that he could do. He was asked to form an association of laypeople who would carry on the brothers' apostolate to those on the margin of society. At first he heard this as a suggestion that he give up his interest in prison justice. Then he saw it as an opportunity to get some people in the Catholic community interested in and involved in prison work. He saw the suggestion as a way he himself could wash more feet instead of expecting the institutional Church to come up with a plan, money and personnel.

The command to serve is but one aspect of a broader command that Jesus gave a little later in his Last Supper talk to his friends: "I give you a new commandment, that you love one another. Just as I have loved you, you also should love one another. By this everyone will know that you are my disciples, if you have love for one another" (13:34-35).

The do's and don'ts for loving service would easily fill volumes because they touch so many of the contacts we have each day with people. Perhaps the easiest way to determine whether we are living the kind of service and love Jesus calls us to live would be to spend a few minutes each evening picturing the Last Supper, seeing Jesus washing feet, hearing his words and recalling the inconvenient little things we have done or not done during the day in response to requests for help, whether explicit or implicit. This image, repeated day after day, would soon determine the way we respond in all our contacts with other people.

Betrayal and Denial

In his drama about the last days of Jesus's life John shows that not all the "bad guys" were Jesus' hecklers or members of the power elite. Right in his own group of close disciples were one who would betray him and one who would deny him: Judas and Peter.

We have a hard time comprehending Judas. How could anyone who had been close to Jesus for three years turn on him for a few measly dollars? It is not quite so hard to appreciate Peter's boastful bravado and his subsequent cowardly denial in face of possible imprisonment, even death. Perhaps we could fathom Judas and Peter a bit better if we reflect on the complex motives that have led us to betray friendship at one time or another.

In any case, Jesus' reaction to the two of them illustrates an essential element of the kind of love he was talking about. Love not being paid back in kind or a person not grasping all the implications of returning love do not justify not extending it freely time and time again. At the very last moment Jesus, by letting Judas know Jesus knew what he had in mind and by telling Peter how he would fail a very important test of friendship, was extending a loving hand to each of them.

FOR REFLECTION

1) *In your own words, how would you describe or define love? What does this definition suggest about the direction your life might take?*

2) *Imagine meeting Jesus and hearing him ask you, "What*

103

*have you done today so that people will know that you
are my disciple?" How will you answer?*

*3) How have you felt and what have you done when a
friend has betrayed your friendship? What does Jesus'
action suggest to you about the way God treats us when
we betray the divine friendship?*

'Fear Not!' (John 14:1—17:26)

Jesus' second command, "Do not let your hearts be
troubled" (14:1a), is no less general, no less difficult than the
first. Fear is an obstacle to living in the light because it casts
such a heavy shadow. It closes down the heart and crushes
the spirit. It distorts one's thinking and turns the will to jelly.
How does one still an anxious heart? How does one put
worry out of mind? How does one remain tranquil when a
loved one is taken away or leaves?

In his Last Supper sermon, Jesus acknowledged that
his friends would have troubles that induce fear. They would
be persecuted, hated, even killed. But he also gave them the
assurance that he would be with them and that they really
had no reason to be afraid to walk in his way.

He did this in several ways. First, he assured them that
he was going to prepare a new home for them, one to which
he is the way. Fear loses some of its enervating power when
we know that there is a home with a loving family always
waiting for us. Anxiety dissipates when the path we are to
take is clear and well-lit. Jesus assured his friends, "And if I
go and prepare a place for you, I will come back again and
will take you to myself, so that where I am, there you may be
also" (14:3). And "I am the way, and the truth, and the life"
(14:6a).

Second, he promised to send a helper, an advocate, one
who would guide them and give them strength. Any trial,
worry or fear loses some of its terror if we have a hand to

hold as we go through it. The helping hand Jesus promised is not only the love and help of the community; it is also the very power and presence of God. He and his Father would send the Spirit of Truth to be with the disciples.

Just as Jesus is the fullness of divinity in the flesh, the Holy Spirit is the fullness of divinity mysteriously present in our midst. Jesus was assuring his disciples that the Godhead will be with them just as truly as he himself was with them, doing for them what he did for them in the flesh.

In the Jewish Scriptures many people experienced and believed in the presence of God among them. But some did not, as the prophets often noted. In the Gospels many people experienced and believed in Jesus, but many did not. In this age when the Spirit is roaming the world, when the Spirit is seeking minds to enlighten, wills to encourage, hearts to warm, some people experience and believe in the Paraclete and many do not. When values clash, when Jesus' absence is keenly felt, when fear of the past, the present and especially of the future immobilizes us, the realization that the Spirit of God is present and active should keep our hearts from being troubled.

Jesus gave his friends a third assurance of help: If they, by love, stay united to him as a branch is united to its vine, they will have all the help they need to deal with and overcome the fears that destroy their inner peace, that weaken their purpose, that induce them to seek the darkness rather than the light, to miss the way and to ignore the truth. "If you abide in me, and my words abide in you, ask for whatever you wish, and it will be done for you" (15:17).

Just as Jesus gave his disciples an example of what service and love mean by washing their feet, so on Good Friday he gave them an example of the ultimate reason why they should not be anxious. At the Last Supper he told them: "But take courage; I have conquered the world!" (16:33c). His conquest of the world—that is, the powers that are opposed to God—would take place in a dramatic way on the cross. The forces of evil would do all that they could do to a human being and he would defeat them, beat them down, conquer them totally. His assurance to his friends was that he would share that victory with them. Thus the command to "fear not" is not as awesome and difficult as it seems.

After this very heavy talk, the disciples must have been confused. Jesus is leaving, yet he tells them not to fear. He is going somewhere they cannot go at present. He is sending a stranger, a Paraclete, to be with them. He is telling them that they are going to have a rough time, but that they should not be anxious. He is assuring them that he will help them.

Then he ends his words by praying for them—praying that they will be united among themselves in love and that they will be one with the Father and with him. "I ask not only on behalf of these, but also on behalf of those who will believe in me through their word, that they may all be one. As you, Father, are in me and I am in you, may they also be in us, so that the world may believe that you have sent me" (17:20-21). As we cry out to God for direction and help in the difficulties of trying to live up to the command to love as Jesus loves and to fear not, Jesus is praying with us and for us. Do we need any more assurance?

Summing Up

In this treatment of John's account of the Last Supper, we have tried to make two points as a framework for our understanding of these chapters and for our prayer arising from them. (1) The commands of the Lord are simple: Love one another and do not fear. (2) We are not alone. Jesus helps us by preparing a place for us, by sending his Spirit to us and by being at our side praying for us as we struggle to walk in the light, to drink the living water and to live a reborn life.

FOR REFLECTION

1) *When you have experienced fear, how has it affected your thinking and feeling? How did you deal with it? Whose hand helped you through it?*

2) *When have you experienced the presence of the Holy Spirit enlightening, guiding and comforting? When you have not been conscious of it, why do you think that is so?*

3) *How does the fact that Jesus prays for us and with us affect our lives?*

4) *What image of God comes to you when you read the words of Jesus at the Last Supper?*

Chapter Nine

'Darkness Has Not Overcome the Light'

IN THE PROLOGUE of his Gospel, John hinted at a confrontation between the Word, who is light, and the forces of darkness. He boldly proclaimed that darkness did not prevail. In John 18—20 he recounts the decisive confrontation between good and evil. In ancient mythologies, when the forces of the good gods braved those of bad gods or of demigods, gigantic battles shook the foundations of the universe. Gods were killed or imprisoned and destructive forces were unleashed on the world.

When *the* battle between good and evil took place, it was in an out-of-the-way corner of the world between a carpenter and a few people whose names hardly appear in the histories of those times. It was the ultimate battle in which the light of pure love dispelled the accumulation of darkness and sin that festered in the very heart of the human race.

At the time of this momentous encounter those present, with the exception of Jesus, did not realize what they were witnessing. No voice from heaven enlightened even friends such as Peter and Judas, who had heard Jesus foretell his passion and death. The high priests, Pilate, the soldiers and the mob were even more blind to the possibility that God might be revealing in this event something of the divine identity and love.

Had a twentieth-century newscaster been there to report, the account would have been short—an account of a lynching. Jesus was seized by a mob. A mock trial determined he should die. Although he was innocent, the authorities acquiesced in the verdict and he was hung on a cross.

Any spectator or participant who even suspected that this was the decisive struggle between good and evil would have thought evil won. The light of the world was extinguished; darkness once again covered the earth as it had before the dawn of creation. But on the third day, with the brilliance of an exploding star, the empty tomb dispelled that darkness and gave light and life to those who had ears to hear and eyes to see.

With this enlightened vision John looked back at the events of Friday from the vantage point of seventy or more years and realized that it had indeed been a *Good* Friday. From the perspective of hindsight John recorded the events of Jesus' last hours.

For John, those events are the final glorification of Jesus as King and Savior, as Son of God. Jesus is the Word, the face of God, the window through which we catch a glimpse of what God is like. Reflecting on the Passion from this viewpoint can be troubling. A God in human flesh whose enemies triumph, whose friends desert him, who dies because of the petty jealousies of some priests and the venality of a judge does not seem to be a very powerful and able God.

If we have an image of God, the sight of whose face could kill, who thunders from mountaintops and destroys all enemies, that image is shattered on Calvary. The image John presents of Jesus, the Son of God, is certainly that of one in control of the situation, but also of one who exercises control in a totally unexpected manner. John's Jesus is not a hapless victim of the powers of darkness. Rather, he takes charge of an unjust situation created by evil and turns it into something dazzlingly good for those who believe. He uses the very means his enemies used to frustrate his work to bring about his plan to enlighten the world.

On the evening of Good Friday, when Jesus' enemies lay down to sleep, they thought that they had triumphed over the troublemaker. But they had, in fact, been the very instruments of testing his devotion and obedience to the Father's will, by which the alienation and disobedience of the human race had been wiped out.

Jesus, Master of the Situation (John 18—19)

John's account of the events in the garden (18:1-11) is remarkably different from that of the other evangelists. He omits the garden's name and place and makes no mention of Jesus' anguished prayer. His Jesus is not a tormented human being crying to his Father for rescue from the coming ordeal. This Jesus knows his purpose and can say to Peter, "Am I not to drink the cup that the Father has given me?" (18:11c). John alone names Peter as the disciple with the sword and Malchus as the slave who lost an ear and was healed by Jesus' touch.

In John, Judas is not the betrayer who identifies Jesus by a kiss. Rather, he shows Jesus taking the initiative and placing himself in the hands of the forces of evil, symbolized by the soldiers and the guards. Jesus asks whom they seek. When they tell him, he answers "I AM." The power of that name, Jesus' power, is shown by the fact that, instead of seizing him, they fall to the ground. He has to repeat his question and again assert his identity before they can take and bind him.

In an incident he inserts at this point, John indicates that Jesus had knowledge of the future, a knowledge that could only be attributable to divine power. At the Last Supper Jesus had foretold that Peter's protestations of faith would not stand up under pressure. He predicted when and how many times Peter would deny him (13:38). Before the cock crows Peter does exactly what Jesus had said he would do (see 18:15-18, 25-27).

Jesus's calm and reasonable answer to Annas and the temple guard who struck him show a man in control of himself under trying circumstances (see 18:19-24). Afterward, at his trial before Pilate, Jesus uses Pilate's questioning to state his purpose for coming into the world and to claim his true kingship. "You say that I am a king. For this was I born, and for this I came into the world, to testify to the truth. Everyone who belongs to the truth listens to my voice" (18:37b). Standing before Pilate, Jesus is confident about who he is and where his strength comes from. Nothing can shake him or deter him from his purpose.

Those who belong to the truth and listen to Jesus share in that purpose. They too are to give testimony to the truth. They too are to know who they are and to be conscious of a strength outside themselves when they testify to the truth. The Jesus John presents is a very powerful person, one who does not use his power the way human beings usually think power should be used, but who is faithful to his mission and accepts the consequences of following that mission with courage and strength.

Beneath the drama of the judge, Pilate, unsuccessfully trying to dismiss the case and being forced by the conniving crowd outside the courtroom to handle the case and ultimately to condemn Jesus to death, we see the struggle between a kingdom that belongs to this world and one that is not from here, between a kingdom based on power and pride and one based on truth and love. The worldly-wise ruler seems to win, but only for about seventy-two hours.

The soldiers put a crown of thorns on Jesus' head and throw a purple cloak over his shoulders, mocking his title as king. They are not aware that this is a decisive moment in human history, that light and truth are battling darkness and lies. But their action reveals in a reverse way the kind of dominion God exercises over the world. The incongruity of a crown made of thorns and an old purple cloak speak of the fact that Jesus' kingship is not one of pomp and power but one of humility and truth.

Unlike the other accounts, John has Jesus carrying his cross alone to Calvary, an indication of his strength and power even after a cruel scourging. Finally, even when Jesus is hanging on the cross in great pain, he still is sufficiently in control to provide for his beloved disciple to care for his mother.

Looking back from the vantage point of Easter and the subsequent activity of the Holy Spirit in the world, we can see that the events John describes are symbolic of divine power working to save God's people.

John makes a point of the fact that it was about noon of Preparation Day for Passover when Pilate handed Jesus over to be crucified. Passover was the great Jewish feast commemorating their escape from bondage in Egypt and safe arrival in the land of Israel. An essential aspect of the feast was the offering of a lamb's blood in the temple. At this hour the temple priests began to slay the Passover lambs. In the beginning of the Gospel, John the Baptizer had pointed Jesus out as the Lamb of God.

The priests who offered the Passover sacrifices wore a special garment. The garment Jesus wore, for which the soldiers cast dice, was seamless, suggesting the deeper meaning of his death—namely, that it was sacrificial and salvific.

John says that as Jesus died "he gave up his spirit" (19:30c). From subsequent events we can easily conclude that more was intended by these words than that Jesus "gave up the ghost." Rather, they suggest that through his death Jesus gave his Spirit, the Holy Spirit, to the world to do what he had promised the Paraclete would do.

Even the placing of Jesus' mother Mary and the beloved disciple at the foot of the cross suggests something momentous is occurring. A new creation is being born. Mary represents the new Eve receiving life from the new Adam

113

and passing it on to her children, the believers represented by John. As the mother who gave physical birth to the Messiah, she represented the people of Israel from whose stock he sprang. Now her motherhood is elevated. She is the spiritual mother of the Church, of the new Israel.

The flow of blood and water from the side of the dead Christ is a clue to the fact that from the death of Jesus flow the living waters of a new life communicated by the Spirit though Baptism and the Eucharist.

The reader of the Passion story can still be blind and not see the deeper reality behind the events. Indifference, self-interest, fear of belief's consequences, even hatred can blind one to the basic question this narrative poses: "What does the narrative reveal to me about God?"

Of course, God's kingship and power are evident. A fitting response is awe: "Our God is like no other god in concern for people!" Gratitude inspires us to exclaim in wonder: "God did this for me?" A sense of closeness and unity is appropriate, because we see a God who is compassionate, who has suffered as we do. We see a God who does not send legions of angels to correct human injustices, but who loves us enough to free us from the sin that keeps us from him even if he has to die for us. We see a God not of awe and majesty, but one who can empathize with the human condition. We see a God of hope in the face of what seems like ultimate and final defeat.

The basic response to this narrative should be belief: "This is the kind of God I can believe in and put my trust in. This is my kind of God!"

FOR REFLECTION

1) *If you are able to recall a time when there was a big struggle between good and evil in your life, what were your feelings at the time? Do you feel that God was with you and brought some good out of the situation for you?*

114

2) At times when you have been misjudged or misunderstood, how confident have you felt about who you are? What gave you the inner strength to stand up for what you believed was right?

3) What difficulties do you experience in seeing God in the suffering Jesus?

Chapter Ten

The Empty Tomb

THE BURIAL OF JESUS should have brought the story of his earthly career to an end. He was placed in a tomb and it was sealed. His band of followers was in disarray. Some had left. Others huddled in fear, disillusioned of their hope that he was the Messiah. The crucifixion had shattered all their dreams that he was the longed-for king who would restore the kingdom of Israel. Were that all there was to Jesus' story, his name would never have made the history books. What caused that name to ring throughout the world for two thousand years, to inspire billions of people to follow him and many thousands to die for him? The reason Jesus is not seen as just another Messianic figure with illusions of grandeur but as the focal point of human history is that he did not stay in that tomb. On the third day he rose, and the disciples experienced him as one who had a new and different kind of life that he shared with them.

There were no eyewitnesses to the Resurrection. There were no photographers waiting for the stone to be rolled away. There is no record of what the guards saw or experienced—if they saw anything at all. But something happened that in record time turned a dispirited group of disciples into enthusiastic, fervent evangelizers.

Some of them had run away when trouble rose. A few had been at Calvary. All realized that Jesus had died; they knew where he had been buried. But suddenly, as he predicted, he once again encountered them, reestablished his relationship with them and sent them out to tell the whole world that he had risen. That one fact caps John's recital of the signs Jesus did so that his readers may come to belief and have life (see 20:30-31). As Paul exclaims, "[I]f Christ has not been raised, then our proclamation has been in vain and your faith has been in vain" (1 Corinthians 15:14).

The four Gospel accounts of Jesus' post-Resurrection appearances leave much to be desired if we want to put them in a consistent, orderly, chronological sequence. The difficulty of finding an exact account of who went to the tomb is illustrated by the four different reports the evangelists give of the women at the tomb.

John writes that only Mary Magdalene went to the tomb (John 20:1). Matthew has her going there in company with "the other Mary" (see Matthew 28:1). Mark names Mary Magdalene, Mary the mother of James and Salome (see Mark 16:1), while Luke places Mary Magdalene, Joanna, Mary the mother of James and "other women" at the tomb (see Luke 24:10).

This confusion becomes a non-question when we realize that all the evangelists were using the basic events to express the belief of the first disciples and the early Christian community that Jesus was indeed alive and involved with them. Jesus rose; he appeared to his disciples, who recognized him; he gave them his Spirit and eventually left them. The disciples believed this, and the faith of all future believers is based on their faith in the Resurrection.

When we read John's account of the events that occurred after the disciples discovered the empty tomb, we can look at them from two different perspectives. One is to concentrate on who said what, where and when. This perspective gives rise to many questions about the accuracy of these incidents and about how they can be reconciled with the Resurrection accounts in the Synoptic Gospels.

The other perspective—John's own—is a theological one, one that through the characters and events captures the meaning that lies behind the events. For John Jesus' glorification, his exaltation and triumph over the forces of darkness, occurred when he died and rose. When he was lifted up on that trunk of a tree and drew his last breath he was, in fact, lifted up in glory to the Father. At that moment he poured out his Spirit so that those who believe might have light and life.

John sees Calvary as the instantaneous transformation of Jesus to a new level of reality, to a new kind of life unlike anything known before. The crucifixion, the resurrection, the giving of the Spirit and the return to the Father form one event undivided by time or place. To help others understand this mystery, John recounts events separated by time and space to show how the disciples came to the same understanding of them as he has.

The disciples' experiences in John 20 are symbolic of the experiences future members of the Christian community will undergo to reach a profound understanding of the mystery of Jesus. The steps seem simple enough: Jesus reveals himself as Lord and the disciple responds by believing. But, as the apostles' bewilderment and lack of understanding illustrates, this belief does not come instantaneously or painlessly. It is born from a sense of the Lord's absence. It is tested by fear and doubt. Finally, the disciple recognizes Jesus and faith cries with Thomas, "My Lord and my God!" (see John 20:28). People do not realize that feeling the absence of Jesus, nagging doubt and even fear of what faith will entail are all part of the process of belief. The key is to be on watch for the revelation of the risen Christ.

'He Is Risen!' (John 20:1-31)

The realization that Jesus is truly alive, risen and in glory comes in different ways to different people. Take, for example, the different reactions of Mary Magdalene, Peter and John.

Mary went to the tomb and found it empty, which did not convey to her the fact that Jesus had risen. She realized that something unexpected had happened, most likely that someone had stolen the body. The empty tomb did not reassure her. It was not a place of revelation for her. Rather it heightened the sense of loss she experienced when Jesus was crucified. Now she could not even be near his corpse.

She went to tell the disciples, who themselves were wracked by fear and doubts, who were mourning the absence of Jesus. Two of them, Peter and the disciple whom Jesus loved ran to the tomb. The fact that the beloved disciple slowed to allow Peter to take the first look says nothing about the primacy of Peter. Rather it is a dramatic way for John to make a point.

Peter looked in, saw the empty tomb and was puzzled. Perhaps he too thought that someone had removed the body. That scenario was not likely, since the napkin that covered Jesus' face was in one place and the winding cloth neatly rolled up in another. No grave robber would have taken the time to unwrap the body and then carefully wind up the burial cloth. (Perhaps John adds this touch to counteract a rumor that the disciples had stolen and hidden the body.)

Peter did not comprehend what he had seen until later. On the other hand, the beloved disciple saw and believed immediately. Even before he understood that Scripture had foretold the Lord's Resurrection, his love made him so sensitive to the Lord's presence that he could believe without seeing. Perhaps the reason there is no physical description of the risen Christ is because he can only be recognized by faith and love.

When the two men returned home, Mary once again went to the garden. She had to see in order to believe. What she saw was not a resuscitated Jesus, but a Jesus who now lived on another plane of reality. She met him in an unfamiliar guise, thought him a gardener and recognized him only when her called her name. Her heart responded to his voice and she threw her arms around him.

He told her to stop holding on to him. This gentle rebuke goes further than a request to let go of him. It was a gentle reminder that she would not have the kind of relationship with him that she had known when he was preaching. He would leave her and the others and be with the Father—but true to his promise, he would be with her and them in a new and different way.

Just how he would be with her and the other disciples in the future is described by John in a tender scene. Mary went back to the others and told them that she had seen and talked to the Lord, but it seems that her testimony did not convince them. They still cowered in fear. Suddenly Jesus was there among them. He greeted them, wishing them peace. The peace he was calling down upon them was more than the absence of conflict in their lives. It was that assurance and confidence that comes when a person knows deep inside that he or she is in tune with God and therefore has no cause to fear anything or anyone.

Jesus showed them his hands and side, but there is no indication that they actually touched him. This action demonstrated that he was the same person they had known for three years. He was the same—there were his pierced hands and side—but he was also different. Solid walls hindered him not.

Without any fanfare, Jesus committed his mission into the hands of his friends: "As the Father has sent me, so I send you" (20:22b). If fear because they were Jesus' friends had caused the disciples to hide behind locked doors, what anxiety must have been in their hearts when they heard these words! There was no way they could preach as fearlessly as he had, no way they could cure as effectively and effortlessly as he had, no way they could love and forgive as generously as he had.

Jesus must have realized the turmoil in their hearts because he showed them how they would do all these things. He gently breathed on them and said, "Receive the Holy Spirit" (20:22b).

The impact of this simple gesture accompanied by four simple words has been barely appreciated through the ages. It harks back to the beginning of the Book of Genesis, when "the LORD God formed man from the dust of the ground, and breathed into his nostrils the breath of life; and the man became a living being" (Genesis 2:7).

Without the Spirit we would have no access to the life the Son came to share with us. Our transformation needs the Spirit doing the work of advocacy, consolation, encouragement and peacemaking. This was the help that Jesus had promised at the Last Supper to give his friends when he left them (see 14:15-27).

These four words—"Receive the Holy Spirit"—that are so essential to understanding how Jesus' disciples can live his life and take on the task the Father entrusted to him are unique to John. None of the other three Gospels mention Jesus bestowing the Holy Spirit.

Mark implies it when Jesus tells his friends not to worry what they will say when dragged into court in his name: "for it is not you who speak, but the Holy Spirit" (Mark 13:11c). Matthew indicates the gift of the Holy Spirit when Jesus sends forth the disciples to baptize all peoples "in the name of the Father and of the Son and of the Holy Spirit" (Matthew 28:19b). Luke merely quotes Jesus as saying that his Father will "give the Holy Spirit to those who ask him!" (Luke 11:13b).

True, in Acts Luke pictures the coming of the Spirit in a roaring wind and tongues of fire, empowering the apostles to speak in tongues. But only in John does Jesus quietly transfer his Spirit, the Holy Spirit, the fullness of divinity, into the hearts of the disciples to empower them to free people from the sins that limit or destroy the life Jesus gives them.

The relatively few references to the Holy Spirit in the Gospels, plus the descriptions of the work of the Spirit in the Letters and the manifestations of the role of the Spirit in the early community reported in Acts are the core on which the

Church has reflected and argued over the centuries. It took the Church three and a half centuries to achieve a clear understanding that the Holy Spirit is true God, equal with the Father and Son, the fullness of divinity just as they are. One of the major theological reasons for the division between the Eastern and the Western Church was the simple phrase *and the Son*. The West inserted the phrase into the Creed, insisting that the Holy Spirit proceeded from the Father *and the Son*; the East said the phrase did not belong there.

This event suggests that often Jesus reveals his face to people in unexpected ways. During World War I a soldier became interested in religion. For twenty years, a time of doubt and questioning, he read and studied books about the Catholic faith. Then one day he suddenly decided the time had come for him to make a decision. He had no vision of Jesus, but that day he "saw" the Lord. He knocked on a rectory door and asked the priest to baptize him.

Along with the bestowal of the Spirit, Jesus gave the apostles the commission to forgive sins. Matthew places the bestowal of the power to forgive sins at a different time and in different circumstances (see Matthew 16:19; 18:18). One explanation is that Jesus did it twice. The commission to forgive or not was not the granting of an arbitrary power, but a restatement of a theme from Jesus' preaching that none are so blind as those who will not see. Being bound comes from the sinners' choice not to change and not to accept the forgiveness and love offered to them through those who share in this power.

In this tableau we can see in dramatic form the power of Jesus to release people from their fears. When Jesus was arrested and executed, the disciples fled in fear for their own safety, locking the door of the room where they gathered. The door is a symbol of the way fear blocks us off from others. Those outside cannot come in and those inside cannot go out. That room was like Lazarus' tomb. Those inside were not physically dead, but they were dead in another way. Their purpose in life, their hopes, their ambitions had died.

As yet they had not heard the voice of Jesus.

Then, just as he had ordered the stone to be rolled from Lazarus' tomb, Jesus opened the grave in which they had buried themselves. Jesus had told the bystanders to unwind Lazarus. Now he gave his friends the peace and strength to overcome their fears and to go out and fulfill the commission he gave them.

How People Accept the Resurrection

In the appearances of Jesus to the disciples in the Upper Room, we see how they (and many people today) react to the Good News of the Resurrection. They did not accept Magdalene's word. Peter and the beloved disciple ran off to see for themselves before they would believe. Today we still meet those who are struggling with the absence of Jesus in their lives, who wallow in fear and doubt, but will not accept the assurance of others that he is alive and is with them.

Thomas is the extreme example of this type. He will not even take the witness of the community. He needs hard proof, his kind of proof, and he gets it. The goodness and love of Jesus, of God, for hardheaded people is all too evident in this little exchange. It is reassuring that the Lord will reveal himself, will give an unmistakable sign to those who want to believe and who do not shun the fellowship of believers even though they have grave and serious doubts.

John's account of the Easter event shows that the faith of the apostles and the first disciples was not based on an empty tomb, but on a powerful encounter with the living and transformed Lord. It also shows how people struggle to believe, as well as the fact that the Lord reveals himself in different ways to different people. There is no one route to the cry of surrender, "My Lord and my God!"

The Final Two Appearances (John 21:1-23)

The final chapter of John's Gospel illustrates the complexity of biblical scholarship. It raises questions of authorship and of purpose. The choice of words, the style of the language and the thought patterns all indicate that someone other than the author of the first twenty chapters added this chapter. Yet it must have been incorporated into the text very early, because it is found in all the earliest manuscripts we have.

The reason for incorporating these events at this point raises questions. For example, it is hard to explain why the disciples were back at their old trade and did not recognize Jesus when he showed up on the shore. After all, they had experienced the Easter event. They had received the Holy Spirit and had been commissioned by Jesus. What more did they need to begin the task he had given them?

Some have suggested that this incident is really Jesus' first appearance to the disciples, not the third. Since the first author did not use it, the author of the epilogue placed it where it is. Others think John has transposed the tradition about the miraculous catch of fish (Luke 5:4-14), where Peter professed his faith. But neither is Luke's story found at the very beginning of Jesus' ministry where the earliest Gospel, Mark, places it. This transposition of stories bewilders people with a keen sense of chronological order. But it is not important when we realize that the evangelists use incidents such as this to make a theological point.

What then is the point of adding this incident and the dialogue between Jesus and Peter as an epilogue? After all, John has already shown that Jesus had manifested his risen presence, was with his heavenly Father, had bestowed the Holy Spirit and had given a charge to the disciples. All of this seems to have been done on that first Easter day instead of over a period of forty days.

Scholars are not sure why these words were added. They do, however, enrich faith because of the meanings we can find in them. For example, Jesus' offering bread to the fishermen suggests the Eucharist.

Some ancient commentators saw symbolism in the number of fish—153—the disciples caught. The fourth-century biblical authority Saint Jerome thought that this was the number of all the known species of fish, hence symbolic of the fact that the apostles were sent to fish for people of every race and nation in the world. Other ancient writers saw the unbroken net as a symbol of the universal mission of the Church: to bring all peoples into unity in Christ.

All these questions and speculations are good because they help us appreciate the complexity of interpreting Scripture and the diversity of answers that are often permissible. Different people will at different times find different spiritual food in these incidents. For example, this breakfast suggests two guiding principles for the disciples of Jesus: (1) Without Jesus we can do nothing. The disciples had worked hard all night and had no fish in their boat. Then Jesus appears and gives them direction; they make a marvelous catch. (2) Jesus is not recognized with bodily eyes but is seen by faith in the Eucharist, the meal where he hands out the bread that he has said is his Body. These two applications should give each reader much material for reflection.

The reason for recording at this point the triple questioning of Peter and his triple affirmation of love is no less perplexing. Peter certainly had been in the Upper Room when Jesus appeared. Saint Paul seems to indicate that Jesus had talked with Peter some time previously: "[Jesus] appeared to Cephas, then to the twelve" (1 Corinthians 15:5). But some writers think that Paul was referring to this incident.

Another possible reason for adding this story here is that when the text ended with Jesus' Easter appearance, people wanted to know what eventually happened to Peter and the beloved disciple. Still others theorize that the framework of the Christian community was gradually emerging, and the author wanted to show that Jesus was present though not visible in that community through the authority of Peter and through the Eucharist.

The writer of the epilogue concludes his narration with Jesus asking three times if Peter loves him and Peter asking Jesus what would happen to the beloved disciple (21:15-23). It is difficult to figure out why Jesus asked the same question twice more after Peter answered clearly and firmly the first time. Perhaps it was to substantiate firmly Peter's love for Jesus in spite of his denials and to show that Jesus gave him a responsibility to match that love. Perhaps the three avowals of love were reparation for the Peter's three denials of Jesus. Perhaps they were repeated for emphasis.

In any case Jesus commissioned Peter to care for the flock with the same kind of love he himself had shown in teaching, guiding and caring for his followers. This segment certainly was written after Peter had been crucified in Rome under Nero about the year A.D. 63, which the community would have known. The writer may have used that fact to show that Jesus had foreknowledge of the kind of death his friend would suffer. "Stretching out one's arms" was an image of crucifixion. Peter was to follow Jesus not to a comfortable old age but to the same kind of death and the same kind of reward.

Peter's question concerning the fate of the beloved disciple and Jesus' answer may have been the author's response to some confusion in the community about the Second Coming of Christ. Jesus had said that some of those who believed in him would not see death until that time but, by the time John wrote, most of the apostolic generation had seen death. Even the beloved disciple had most likely died. Jesus' words that the time and place are of no concern to Peter was a warning to those who would like to set conditions for the Second Coming.

The only important thing is to love and follow the Lord, whether it be in a heroic way that gives witness by martyrdom or in the more quietly heroic way of being a truthful and faithful witness within the community. Jesus' question, "[W]hat is that to you?" (21:23d), seems to imply that each person has a unique calling and should not worry about how others are called. There is no place for competition and jealousy among the followers of Jesus.

FOR REFLECTION

1) *In your own reflection on the life of Jesus, in what order would you rank the importance of these events: his birth, his preaching, his miracles, his death, his resurrection/ascension?*

2) *Recall a time when you "saw" the Lord—that is, came to realize that he was alive and with you. What occurred and how did you feel?*

3) *On what do you base your belief that Jesus has risen from the dead?*

4) *Summarize the image of God you discovered in this Gospel. How is it like or different from the one you had before you began to reflect on John's Gospel?*

Conclusion

The Gospel of John emphasizes the divinity of Jesus more than the other Gospels. God is made visible in Jesus. The God we see in John is almost too good to be true.

Human beings have always had to describe their deities in human terms and have attributed human characteristics to them. Thus, various gods have been lustful, adulterers, thieves, murderers and drunks, often indifferent to the human condition. The God of the Israelites was different. When the Word became flesh and pitched his tent among us, he showed the face of a God who is caring, concerned and present to the human situation. This God freely entered the human situation, including death, and even allowed people the freedom to turn away and in so doing to condemn themselves.

Jesus revealed a God who has all of the most noble characteristics humans can think of, a God who is almost too good to be true, who *is* pure love. This image of God unfolded most clearly in the rich tradition of the community that grew up around the beloved disciple, the one whom Jesus loved best. This Gospel is witness to that tradition and it has the authority, the veracity, the understanding of that disciple and of the Church as its guarantee of truthfulness.

FOR REFLECTION

A good way to end this brief study of John's Gospel is to reflect on the book as a whole and ask how it touched, enlightened and motivated us. The answers to these questions will reveal how much we have been able to look beneath the surface recital of events and find the bright Light shining in the darkness.

1) *Did the account get under your skin in such a way as to trouble you about some things you have held in the past to be certain, or to raise old questions you thought settled? In other words, did all or parts of it shake you up and move your heart?*

2) *Did the narrative provide meaning for your life and give it direction? How? By helping you understand what life is all about, by offering companionship in your pain, by changing the basic way you look at life, by suggesting areas for education and development?*

3) *Did John's soaring vision energize you to action, to movement in the direction it indicates? If so, what action or actions did you take?*

4) *In what way did this study help you answer the*

question at the beginning of the book: What do you hope to get from this book?

For Further Reading

To break open a Gospel, one needs to read more than one commentary as well as the Gospel itself. The following volumes may provide helpful insights to the reader.

Flanagan, Neal M. *The Gospel According to John and the Johannine Epistles*. Collegeville, Minn.: The Liturgical Press, 1989.

McBride, Alfred, O. Praem. *The Divine Presence of Jesus: Meditation and Commentary on the Gospel of John*. Huntington, Ind.: Our Sunday Visitor Publishing, 1992.

Obach, Robert E., and Kirk, Albert. *The Commentary on the Gospel of John*. Mahwah, N.J.: Paulist Press, 1981.

Senior, Donald, C.P. *The Passion of Jesus and John*. Collegeville, Minn.: The Liturgical Press/Michael Glazier, 1991.